Differentiated Supervision

2nd Edition

Allan A. Glatthorn

Association for Supervision and Curriculum Development
Alexandria, Virginia

Association for Supervision and Curriculum Development
1250 N. Pitt Street • Alexandria, Virginia 22314-1453
Telephone: 1-800-933-2723 or 703-549-9110 • Fax: 703-299-8631

Gene R. Carter, *Executive Director*
Michelle Terry, *Assistant Executive Director, Program Development*
Ronald S. Brandt, *Assistant Executive Director*
Nancy Modrak, *Managing Editor, ASCD Books*
Margaret A. Oosterman, *Associate Editor*
Jayne Castelli, *Copyeditor*
Mary Jones, *Project Assistant*
Gary Bloom, *Manager, Design and Production Services*
Karen Monaco, *Designer*
Tracey A. Smith, *Production Coordinator*
Valerie Sprague, *Desktop Publisher*

ASCD publications present a variety of viewpoints. The views expressed or implied
in this book should not be interpreted as official positions of the Association.

Printed in the United States of America.

ASCD Stock No. 196247
ASCD member price: $13.95; nonmember price: $16.95
s1/97

Library of Congress Cataloging-in-Publication Data
Glatthorn, Allan A., 1924-
    Differentiated supervision / Allan A. Glatthorn. — 2nd ed.
      p. cm.
    Includes bibliographical references.
    ISBN 0-87120-275-1
    1. School supervision—United States. 2. Teachers—In-service
training—United States. I. Title.
LB2806.4.G548 1997
371.2'03'0973—dc21   96-45895
                                             CIP

01   00   99   98   97   5   4   3   2   1

About the Author

Allan A. Glatthorn is a Distinguished Research Professor in the School of Education, East Carolina University. He was a professor at the University of Pennsylvania and also served as a high school teacher and principal for many years. Author of more than 20 professional books, he has consulted with more than 100 school systems in helping them develop their own versions of differentiated supervision.

Glatthorn can be reached at the School of Education, East Carolina University, Speight Building, Greenville, NC 27858-4353.

Differentiated Supervision, 2nd edition

Acknowledgments

This book is the result of collaboration on several fronts. First, I have continued to benefit from input provided by my graduate students at East Carolina University; they have brought a measure of needed practicality to my theoretical recommendations. Charles R. Coble, Dean of the School of Education, has been a consistent supporter of my work and has provided the kind of leadership that all authors need. And for many years now, Ron Brandt has generously encouraged me to write this work and others developed under his aegis; he and his staff have provided the kind of critical judgment that transforms educational jargon into readable prose.

Finally, I owe a significant debt of gratitude to the educators in the schools and school systems who shared with me their experiences and their own models of differentiated supervision. (See the Appendix for their names and addresses.) Their successes attest to the feasibility of the model and their own professional skill. Special thanks are owed to Joan Sando, Principal of the Santa Margarita Elementary School (California), and Marcia Craft-Tripp, Director of Special Education for the Beaufort County (North Carolina schools), both of whom generously shared with me the results of their excellent dissertations.

I dedicate this book to my brothers and sisters, my wife, and my children; all of them have been "family" in the best sense of that term.

—Allan A. Glatthorn

The Foundations of
Differentiated Supervision

1

A Rationale for and an Overview of Differentiated Supervision

Differentiated supervision is an approach to supervision that provides teachers with options about the kinds of supervisory and evaluative services they receive. Although many local variations exist, depending upon district resources and needs, in general, the differentiated model provides intensive development to nontenured teachers and to tenured teachers with serious problems. The rest of the faculty receive options about how they foster their professional development: Most work in collaborative teams in the cooperative development mode; some work with a self-directed approach. In addition, the evaluation processes are differentiated, depending upon tenure status and competence.

This chapter presents a rationale for differentiated supervision and briefly describes each of its components. The next chapter explains the foundation elements all teachers need so the model works effectively. Succeeding chapters explain how each of the options works; the final chapter explains how a school district can design, implement, and evaluate its own model of differentiated development.

A Rationale for Differentiated Supervision

A rationale for differentiated supervision can be seen by examining the issue from four perspectives: the profession, the organization, the supervisor, and the teacher.

The Profession

This perspective emphasizes the importance of professionalizing teaching. If teaching is to become more of a profession and teachers are to be empowered, then they must have more options for supervision. Too often, clinical supervision is offered from a "one-up" vantage point: The supervisor, who has the solution, will help the teacher, who has the problem. Such a perspective sees teaching as a craft, not a profession. Even an experienced teacher is seen as operating at the level of craft, needing feedback from a supervisor about the specific methods of instruction. To understand the folly of such a position, consider how absurd it would seem in the field of surgery: The skilled surgeon is operating, with a "supervisor" taking notes on how the surgeon holds the scalpel, makes the incision, and completes the suturing.

Differentiated supervision operates on the belief that teaching is a profession. As members of a profession, teachers should have more control over their professional development, within generally accepted professional standards. As skilled professionals, they need both support and feedback, but from colleagues and students—not always from administrators or supervisors.

The Organization

No direct evidence exists that schools using differentiated systems are more effective than those using only the standard clinical approach. The argument can be made indirectly, however.

First, evidence shows that more effective schools have a special climate—one that might be characterized with the global term "collegiality." As McLaughlin and Yee (1988) note, a collegial environment provides multiple opportunities for interactions and creates expectations that colleagues will serve as sources of feedback and support. Such an environment, they note, serves as an essential source of teacher stimulation and motivation. And as Van Maanen and Barley (1984) observe, commitment to high standards of performance is more easily promoted through shared professional norms than by bureaucratic controls.

One of the best ways to foster collegiality is with a differentiated system that strongly emphasizes cooperation and mutual assistance. A key component of the differentiated approach enables teachers to work together, helping each other grow professionally. Evidence from several case studies of this approach suggests that teachers involved in such programs feel a greater spirit of cooperation and trust of other teachers (Glatthorn 1984).

The Supervisor

Supervisors need a realistic solution to the problem of finding time for effective supervision. The typical supervisor spends about three hours a week on classroom observation and inservice education. (See Sullivan's 1982 study for data on supervisory time allocations.) In a 36-week school year, the supervisor could devote approximately 100 hours to instructional supervision—enough time to provide clinical supervision to only 10 teachers if the supervisor followed the experts' guidelines. However, most supervisors have much heavier loads. As a result, they compromise by making only one or two observations of most classroom teachers. According to a study by Badiali and Levin (1984) of Pennsylvania supervisors, almost half the supervisors surveyed reported observing teachers only once or twice a year; 44 percent of those observations lasted for 30 minutes or less. Differentiated supervision enables the supervisor to focus clinical efforts on those teachers needing or requesting them, rather than providing perfunctory, ritualistic visits for all teachers.

The Teacher

Several arguments can be advanced from the teachers' perspective. First, as Burden (1990) concluded, teachers' preferences for developmental assistance vary, depending upon their stages of professional development. While novices seem to value the intensive assistance of clinical supervision, more advanced teachers prefer options that respond to their individual needs.

Second, competent, experienced teachers do not need intensive development. They have the necessary basic skills to do a competent job in their day-to-day teaching. If a new program is implemented requiring the mastery of new skills, then staff development supported by peer coaching has proved effective. And informal observations can give these teachers the ongoing feedback they need.

Finally, the research provides convincing evidence that with the right types of organizational support, teachers can learn from experienced colleagues. Little (1988) concludes from her studies that teachers welcome and profit from qualified observers, either peers or administrators, who will not waste the teacher's time, who will not insult the teacher's intelligence, and who will work as hard to understand classroom events as the teachers do to conduct them.

Components of Differentiated Supervision

Differentiated supervision includes three developmental options and two evaluative options.

The Developmental Options

"Developmental options" is used here to mean the choices teachers have in fostering their professional development. Three options are provided:

• *Intensive development* is this author's special approach to "clinical supervision." Typically, all nontenured teachers must participate in intensive development; also, tenured teachers who appear to have serious instructional problems are expected to work in the intensive mode. In this author's approach, the intensive development is provided by a supervisor, an administrator, or a mentor. The supervisor (a term used here to include all who provide the intensive development) observes, analyzes, confers, and coaches, working with the teacher toward significant growth. Throughout a school year, the supervisor and the teacher might use as many as seven cycles of the basic processes. All their work is focused solely on improving student learning; teaching methods are seen as means to an end, not an end unto themselves.

• *Cooperative development* is a developmental option in which small groups of teachers work together to help each other develop professionally. Typically, teachers' professional growth is directly related to their school's improvement plan. To support school improvement and to nurture their mutual growth, these teachers use a variety of strategies. They hold professional dialogues, conduct action research, observe and confer with each other, and develop curriculum and learning materials.

• *Self-directed development* enables teachers to work independently, in a sense, supervising themselves. While the principal supports the teacher working in this mode, the teacher typically sets a growth goal, undertakes actions to accomplish the goal, gets feedback from students, and makes a final assessment of progress. In these ways, a teacher directs individual growth without relying upon a supervisor or colleagues.

The Evaluative Options

The differentiated development system seems to work better with two evaluative options:

• *Intensive evaluation* is provided to all teachers working in intensive development. The intensive evaluation is used to make high-stakes decisions: grant tenure, deny tenure; promote, not promote; and renew contract, not renew contract. An intensive evaluation is based upon specific research-supported criteria; involves several observations and conferences; evaluates performance of the noninstructional functions; and is typically carried out by a school administrator.

• *Standard evaluation* is provided to the rest of the teachers. Because these teachers are experienced and known to be competent, this evaluation uses the minimum number of observations and conferences specified by state or district policies and is solely a compliance mechanism to satisfy policy requirements.

Concluding Note

Differentiated supervision is not offered as one more remedy for education's ills. However, the following chapters illustrate that it can exert a positive influence on the professional development of teachers—which is instrumental in achieving school improvement. Schools can improve without the differentiated model—but they have a better chance if they provide teachers with options for growth.

References

Badiali, B., and J. Levin. (April 1984). "Supervisors' Responses to the Survey." Paper presented at the annual meeting of the American Educational Research Association, New Orleans. (ERIC Document Reproduction Service No. 259 456).

Burden, P.R. (1990). "Teacher Development." In *Handbook of Research on Teacher Education*, edited by W.E. Houston. New York: Macmillan, pp. 311-328.

Glatthorn, A.A. (1984). *Differentiated Supervision*. Alexandria, Va.: Association for Supervision and Curriculum Development.

Little, J.W. (1988). "Assessing the Prospects for Teacher Leadership." In *Building a Professional Culture in Schools,* edited by A. Lieberman. New York: Teachers College Press, pp. 78-106.

McLaughlin, M.W., and S.M. Yee. (1988). "School as a Place to Have a Career." In *Building a Professional Culture in Schools,* edited by A. Lieberman. New York: Teachers College Press, pp. 23-42.

Sullivan, C.G. (March 1982). "Supervisory Expectations and Work Realities: The Great Gulf." *Educational Leadership* 39, 6: 448-451.

Van Maanen, J., and S.R. Barley. (1984). "Occupational Communities." In *Research in Organizational Behavior,* edited by S.R. Barley. Greenwich, Conn.: JAI Press, pp. 287-365.

2

Developing the Foundations for Differentiated Supervision

Any effective supervision system must be developed on firm professional foundations: Supervision, like other functions of schooling, is sensitive to the organizational environment. This chapter explains the foundation elements necessary for the differentiated model.

A Professional Culture

"Culture" is used here to mean the core values and related norms that characterize the organization. Some evidence shows that, in less effective schools, cliques of teachers create their own subcultures; Owens (1987) notes that in the high school he studied, several subcultures existed, each with its own set of norms and values. Johnson (1990) also discovered that the secondary department plays a key role in such fragmentation. However, more effective schools have a strong consensus around the core values despite the existence of friendship groups among the faculty. (See Hill, Foster, and Gendler 1990.)

9

Three values seem especially crucial in supporting the differentiated system:

• **Collaboration.** In a school that values collaboration, administrators and teachers see themselves as partners in fostering student learning. The spirit is of wanting to work together rather than choosing adversarial positions. The principal models cooperation, facilitates cooperative work, and rewards teachers who cooperate. Teachers share materials and exchange ideas.

When such values and their related practices are common throughout the school, collaborative systems of supervision take root easily. When collaborative systems are imposed on teachers in a culture that fosters isolation, the result is what Hargreaves (1994) calls "contrived collegiality," an ineffective system with the form of cooperation but without the substance. As this author has discovered in working with schools interested in the differentiated model, a culture that rewards isolation and competition provides an inhospitable environment for the differentiated model.

• **Inquiry.** When inquiry is a widely shared value, differentiated systems work better because they are premised on the assumption that inquiring about professional practice is a hallmark of professionalism. In the school that values asking and answering questions, the principal and the teachers see themselves as reflective practitioners. They assertively look for problems, pose difficult questions for themselves, build the knowledge base, reflect and use metacognition, and see evaluation as an essential part of the change process.

In a little-known work that deserves wider reading even today, Schaefer (1967) put it this way:

> Teaching, more than any other vocation, perhaps, ought both
> to permit and to encourage the pursuit of meaning beyond
> any current capacity to understand (p. 59).

In the differentiated model, teaching is seen as a continuing search for meaning, one that poses and finds tentative answers to the fundamental questions that confront all educators.

• **Continuous Improvement.** Those who commit to continuous improvement see change as a journey, not a destination. Rather than seeking one final solution to education's problems, they understand that continuous incremental change is the road to excellence. They know that the curriculum will always need revising and updating. They realize that teaching can always be improved. They understand that school and classroom climate is always in need of fine tuning.

Continuous improvement is critical in the area of instruction. New technology facilitates students' problem solving. New knowledge about teaching and learning will continue to be produced, suggesting the need to acquire new models of teaching. Students from troubled backgrounds present new challenges to all teachers. As Fullan (1991) determined from his review of the research on the change process, the most effective schools were those that committed themselves to incremental change and continuous improvement.

Supportive Work Conditions

Teachers need a work environment that both manifests and supports their professionalism. A review of the research on the work environment factors that seem most important to teachers suggests two sets of factors: essential elements and enriching elements. (See especially Corcoran 1990.)

Essential Elements

The essential elements might be seen as the basics of the work environment that must be in place for teachers to work effectively. An analysis of the survey results reviewed by Corcoran suggests that five such elements can be identified:

• **Salaries.** First, teachers should earn salaries that reflect their importance to society. Even though most teachers are not motivated by merit pay, they do want salaries commensurate with their preparation and their responsibilities. Several teacher surveys conclude that teachers believe that improving teacher salaries should be a major goal of programs to improve the schools.

11

• **Physical Environment.** Teachers must feel they work in a safe, orderly, and comfortable physical environment. And the prevalence of violence in the schools—much of it directed at teachers—makes safety the most important issue of all. One study of 31 urban schools concluded that many of these schools were dreary, crowded, and in a state of poor repair (Corcoran, White, and Walker 1988).

• **Instructional and Professional Resources.** Teachers need two kinds of resources. First, they need resources for effective student learning: quality learning materials, attractive classrooms, and up-to-date technology. Second, they need professional books, journals, and access to electronic databases that will support their professional growth.

• **Time.** Teachers need time to plan, produce materials, carry out action research, and give each other feedback. This high-quality time is critical if collaboration is to occur.

Schools have solved the problem of time in a variety of ways. Some arrange schedules so that all teachers in a given department or team have common preparation periods. Others hire aides or use volunteers to cover classes. Some schedule student assemblies or large-group presentations so most teachers are freed from instructional responsibilities for a brief period. Other schools start late or dismiss early. All such compromises erode instructional time, of course, and must be used in moderation.

• **Teachable Assignments.** Teachers should teach subjects in their own areas of expertise and not have more than two preparations. They should have a room of their own, if possible, and classes that are not exceptionally difficult to instruct. Large numbers of disruptive students and special needs students representing a wide range of abilities present special instructional problems. Class size should be reasonable. In a large-scale study, 53 percent of the K–6 teachers surveyed reported that "overcrowded classes" was either a "very serious" or "somewhat serious" problem (Louis Harris and Associates 1995). Although the research on the relationship between class size and student achievement is inconclusive, a recent study has shown that K–3 students in classes of 13–17 students made significantly higher scores on standardized achievement tests in the basic areas of the curriculum, as compared with students in both regular and large classes. Those same students sustained their improvement through the middle school years (Achilles, Nye, and Zaharias 1995).

Enriching Elements

Once the essential elements are in place, enriching elements provide even stronger sources of motivation for effective teaching:

• **Learning-Centered Leadership.** The principal keeps the central mission of the school in the forefront and takes action to accomplish that mission. The complex issue here is for the principal to empower teachers through team leadership without abdicating the principal's authority. Studies of effective principals indicate that they have found ways of increasing teacher power while maintaining their role as instructional leader. While the principal works with a leadership team and a central decision-making body, the principal maintains an active role as instructional leader.

The research suggests that the following principal behaviors are vital in executing such a role (the summary draws from several sources: Lee 1987, Smith and Andrews 1989, Blase and Kirby 1992, Sergiovanni 1992, and Cunningham and Gresso 1993):

♦ Shape the school culture to embody and support learning-centered values.

♦ Articulate a vision of excellence and enable others to share effectively in the visioning process.

♦ Recognize the moral dimensions of schooling, act ethically, and sensitize teachers and students to the moral aspects of teaching and learning.

♦ Maintain a focus on curriculum and instruction by informing teachers of current developments, sharing knowledge gained from experience, observing teachers at work, monitoring the implementation of the curriculum, and rewarding effective teaching.

♦ Use routine activities and informal interactions to reinforce teacher commitment to learning.

♦ Use persuasion and influence to improve the quality of learning, while using formal authority as needed.

♦ Create a climate of high expectations for everyone, while assisting teachers in acquiring new skills; supporting teachers in disciplinary matters; and building a developmentally appropriate school curriculum.

♦ Secure additional resources and allocate resources in a way that best accomplishes organizational goals. Defend instructional time, mobilize special personnel as needed, and build a learning-centered schedule.

♦ Use a problem-solving approach to foster continuing improvement. Evaluate formatively and summatively, investigate problems, use reflection to gain insight into problems, and use structures that enable others to become involved in the problem-solving process.

♦ Provide services and structures that foster professional growth to the faculty and to individuals.

♦ Communicate effectively, giving earned and timely praise to all who merit it.

♦ Ensure a safe, orderly, and learning-focused school climate.

♦ Involve parents to enlist their support, to aid them in providing a supportive learning environment, and to use their insights and talents to improve the schools.

• **Meaningful Work.** Some administrators and much of the public, unfortunately, view teachers as mechanics who deliver packaged instruction in a standard manner. Such attempts to de-skill teaching rob the role of purpose and meaning: Teachers in such situations feel like easily replaceable parts. Any supervisory system that succeeds must embrace a contrary view that sees teachers as highly skilled professionals in a demanding, multifaceted, and complex role. Besides teaching effectively, the best teachers develop curriculums, write learning materials, perform action research, provide leadership in problem solving and decision making, counsel troubled students, and involve parents in the classroom.

Even though such tasks can result in role overload, they also help make teaching a meaningful and exciting career, one whose psychic rewards are more powerful than the extrinsic ones.

Facilitating Structures

The facilitating structures are groups (such as committees and task forces) that ensure the effective operation of the differentiated model, with an emphasis on teacher involvement in decision making. Although each school will have its own structure, the following types are recommended for consideration:

• *The instructional teams* are the basic structure for both teaching and decision making; as noted in later chapters, the instructional team will also be useful as the locus of professional development. Elementary and middle schools will probably organize teams by grade level; high schools, by departments or interdepartmental teams. As McLaughlin (1994) notes, the team or department is the natural location for teachers to reflect on their teaching, collaborate on instructional projects, and learn together.

• *The central decision-making body* is a leadership team that uses input from the faculty and its members' own knowledge and experience to identify problems, appoint special task forces, and make critical decisions. In some schools, this is the principal's cabinet; in others, the school improvement team. The name is unimportant, but the function is. The group will be composed largely of teachers, although some schools include all leaders of the instructional teams.

• *Special task forces* are appointed by the central group once a major problem has been identified. A task force has the specific responsibility of studying the problem and developing solutions, which the central group will review and then present to the faculty. The task force is the chief means of addressing interdepartmental or cross-team issues. For example, a task force on teachers' professional development would be responsible for drafting the initial guidelines for the differentiated program.

• *Faculty and team meetings* should be devoted to two major purposes: professional development, and problem identification and solution. These meetings can bring teachers up-to-date on current research and help them examine current issues. They also are the best means for identifying problems and reviewing the solutions proposed by the task forces. In leading these meetings, the principal should avoid premature vote taking, which only increases divisiveness. Instead, the principal should use the meeting as an opportunity to build consensus among the faculty.

These facilitating structures for involvement will give every teacher an opportunity to participate in decision making, without burdening them with administrative responsibilities.

An Understanding of Classroom Complexity

All those involved in teacher development should have a broad understanding of the complexity of the classroom, especially how elements of classroom life affect teacher performance. In too many cases, the administrator or supervisor mistakenly assumes that learning problems are the teacher's fault. As Figure 2.1 shows, several complex factors interact to produce a given classroom performance.

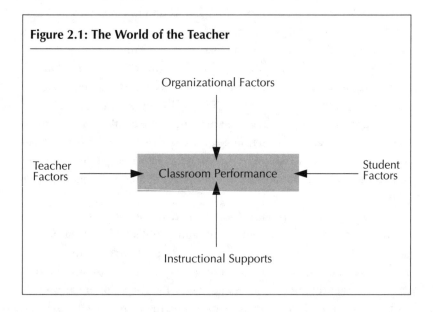

Figure 2.1: The World of the Teacher

Organizational Factors

Teacher Factors → Classroom Performance ← Student Factors

Instructional Supports

Organizational Factors

The organization exercises a strong influence on teacher performance. As noted earlier in this chapter, school culture and teacher work conditions will influence the kind of lesson the teacher presents. If the school values high test scores and teacher accountability, the teacher will respond by teaching to the test in a way that seems ethical to the teacher. And the teacher with four different preparations is likely to plan less than the teacher with one or two.

Student Factors

Observers are usually aware of how the teacher is influencing students; unfortunately, they are less aware that classroom influence is a reciprocal matter. Students influence the teacher in a variety of ways. (See Doyle 1986 for an excellent review of these factors.) First, the relatively large number of students (many with special needs) means that disruption is always possible; thus, the teacher is concerned with management problems, often to the neglect of instruction. Second, the students' varying developmental levels and abilities place a special burden on teachers who try to accommodate the needs of all students. Also, the presence of cliques and gang members in the class makes it essential for the teacher to be sensitive to peer norms. Finally, the level of student motivation is critical. If students are not motivated to learn a particular subject, the teacher may try to make class work easy and entertaining.

Instructional Supports

Three instructional supports clearly affect the teacher's performance on any given day: (1) the district curriculum guide, (2) the textbooks, and (3) the tests. Although the evidence suggests that teachers do not use the district curriculum guides as specific prescriptions for what to teach, they do consult the guides for general guidance, as Clark and Elmore (1981) determined. Thus, a 5th grade teacher presenting a lesson on grammatical terminology may be teaching that useless content simply because the guide prescribes it.

The text is only one of several sources that teachers use to determine what and how to teach. However, for elementary teachers (who must teach several subjects) especially, the text is important. And, as Borko and Niles (1987) note, reliance upon the text may negatively affect the quality of instruction. Textbook series are often repetitious from grade to grade, introduce too many new concepts, and present a shallow treatment of the subject.

State and district tests have a profound influence on what and how the teacher teaches. If teachers are held accountable for students' performance on curriculum-referenced tests, they will emphasize test content and spend much time having students practice on test-like items.

Teacher Factors

In addition to teachers' skills, two other elements play a crucial role in performance. First, several studies conclude that teachers' knowledge affects classroom performance. This knowledge is of four types: subject matter content, including concepts and their relationships; the ability to make content knowledge accessible to students (pedagogical content knowledge); the curriculum, especially what is taught in preceding and succeeding grades; and students, their needs, predispositions, and abilities. Thus, a teacher who sees mathematics as simply a collection of calculation processes will teach it that way, ignoring the richer conceptual understandings.

Second, the teacher's level of motivation will clearly affect classroom performance. A teacher low in motivation is unlikely to plan extensively, assign written work, or use activities that require a great deal of teacher creativity and energy.

The importance of this discussion is clear: Supervisors should understand classroom complexity and examine all factors that might account for a lack of learning, instead of looking only at the teacher's skills.

Comprehensive Services

All teachers need three types of supportive services, which should be provided with a clear understanding of the complexity of the classroom: informal observations, school-based staff development, and frequent interaction with the principal.

Informal Observations

First, principals should make frequent and informal visits to the classrooms. Such observations only need to be 5 to 10 minutes long. The principal drops in; makes an initial scan of the learning processes at work, noting how many students seem on task; and then observes what the teacher is doing to facilitate learning. Many principals have found that a "no-carbon-required" form is useful in giving the teacher prompt feedback. It looks like the form shown in Figure 2.2.

Figure 2.2: Sample Informal Observation Form

On **December 10,** I briefly visited your **math** class.

I liked the way small groups were solving a meaningful problem.

I had a question about why two boys were working at the back

of the room on their own; they did not seem engaged in the task.

Date: December 11, 1996 **Signature:** [Jeffrey Lawson, Principal]

These informal observations serve many purposes. They provide the principal with an opportunity to give the teacher specific, timely, and merited praise; they enable the principal to make an informal assessment of curriculum implementation; and they help the principal stay highly visible, a behavior that teachers value. Also, the "informals" serve as a "distant early warning" signal of emerging problems. For example, if the principal makes three informal observations and each time the teacher sits at the desk while students complete drill-and-practice sheets, a conference would be needed. These observations, however, should not be used in the formal teacher evaluation system because they are so brief and unstructured.

The informal observations are so essential that principals should block out a time each day for such purposes. How much time is reserved will depend, of course, on the size of the faculty; in most schools, one hour a day would be sufficient. At the end of one week, a principal who has set aside an hour daily would have observed at least 20 teachers. Readers interested in learning more about informal observations should consult Frase (1990).

School-Based Staff Development

Second, all teachers need effective staff development at the school level. "Staff development" is used here to denote organized learning experiences for groups of teachers. During the past few years, a new model of staff development has been maturing, one quite different from the skill-focused direct instruction model. Experts are now recommending that this new model be implemented, with the following features (Little 1993, Gall and Vojtek 1994, Lieberman 1995, Darling-Hammond and McLaughlin 1995):

• **Reflective.** Staff development emphasizes reflection and inquiry as teachers work with the principal to solve emerging problems.

• **Relevant.** Sessions connect with the contexts of teaching by focusing on issues of student learning.

• **Collaborative.** Sessions involve professionals holding multiple roles, such as school administrators, district supervisors, counselors, and social workers. They work together to deal with schoolwide issues.

• **Intensive and On-Going.** Instead of one-shot meetings with a consultant, the staff development program aims at depth of teacher learning on a continuing basis.

• **Connected.** Staff development programs link with other developmental strategies so that what happens in the cooperative mode, for example, builds upon and feeds into the staff development sessions.

Frequent Interaction with the Principal

Third, all teachers need structured opportunities to meet with the principal—to exchange ideas, to identify concerns, and to share views of current issues. Principals can satisfy this need in several ways: by meeting periodically with teams and departments; by holding informal seminars before school, during lunch, and during teachers' unscheduled time; and by reserving a portion of each faculty meeting for such exchanges.

The principal should remember the importance of routine as a means of strengthening professional relationships. As Leithwood (1992) observes, effective principals accept the fragmented nature of their role and use many informal and seemingly routine interactions to emphasize everyday factors that impinge upon learning. Thus, a principal monitoring students as they move through the corridors between periods can stop to talk briefly with a teacher about the importance of corridor traffic as a site for potential disruption.

Growth Opportunities Outside the School

As Darling-Hammond and McLaughlin (1995) note, teachers also need several types of growth experiences outside the school. Such opportunities include school/university collaborations; teacher-to-teacher and school-to-school networking, using the computer; partnerships with neighborhood youth organizations; and involvement in growth activities sponsored by the district, the state, and professional organizations.

Concluding Note

No form of supervision used alone in a hostile environment can make a difference in the professional growth of teachers. Professional growth is so complex that it requires a systemic approach in a supportive environment.

References

Achilles, C.M., B. Nye, and J.B. Zaharias. (April 1995). "Policy Use of Research Results: Tennessee's Project Challenge." Paper presented at annual meeting of the American Educational Research Association, San Francisco, Calif.

Blase, J., and P.C. Kirby. (1992). *Bringing Out the Best in Teachers.* Newbury Park, Calif.: Corwin.

Borko, H., and J.A. Niles. (1987). "Descriptions of Teacher Planning." In *Educators' Handbook: A Research Perspective,* edited by V. Richardson-Koehler. New York: Longman, pp. 167–187.

Clark, C.M., and J.L. Elmore. (1981). *Transforming Curriculum in Mathematics, Science, and Writing.* East Lansing, Mich.: Institute for Research on Teaching, Michigan State University.

Corcoran, T.B. (1990). "Schoolwork: Perspectives on Workplace Reform." In *The Contexts of Teaching in Secondary Schools,* edited by M.W. McLaughlin, J.E. Talbert, and N. Bascia. New York: Teachers College Press, pp. 142–166.

Corcoran, T.B., J.L. White, and L. Walker. (1988). *Working in Urban Schools.* Washington, D.C.: Institute for Educational Leadership.

Cunningham, W.G., and D.W. Gresso. (1993). *Cultural Leadership: The Culture of Excellence in Education.* Boston: Allyn and Bacon.

Darling-Hammond, L., and M.W. McLaughlin. (1995). "Policies that Support Professional Development in an Era of Reform." *Phi Delta Kappan* 76, 8: 597–604.

Doyle, W. (1986). "Classroom Organization and Management." In *Handbook of Research on Teaching,* 3rd ed., edited by M.C. Wittrock. New York: Macmillan, pp. 392–421.

Frase, L.E. (1990). *School Management by Walking Around.* Lancaster, Pa.: Technomic.

Fullan, M.G. (1991). *The New Meaning of Educational Change,* 2d ed., New York: Teachers College Press.

Gall, M.D., and R.O. Vojtek. (1994). *Planning for Effective Staff Development: Six Research-Based Models.* Eugene, Oreg.: ERIC Clearinghouse on Educational Management, University of Oregon.

Hargreaves, A. (1994). "Restructuring Restructuring: Postmodernity and the Prospects for Educational Change." In *Teacher Development and the Struggle for Authenticity,* edited by P.P. Grimmett and J. Neufeld. New York: Teachers College Press, pp. 52–82.

Hill, P.T., G.E. Foster, and T. Gendler. (1990). *High Schools with Character.* Santa Monica, Calif.: RAND.

Johnson, S.M. (1990). *Teachers at Work: Achieving Success in Our Schools.* New York: Basic Books.

Lee, G.V. (1987). "Instructional Leadership in a Junior High School: Managing Realities and Creating Opportunities." In *Instructional Leadership: Concepts, Issues, and Controversies,* edited by W. Greenfield. Boston: Allyn and Bacon, pp. 75-99.

Leithwood, K.A. (1992). "The Principal's Role in Teacher Development." In *Teacher Development and Educational Change,* edited by M. Fullan and A. Hargreaves. Washington, D.C.: Falmer, pp. 86-103.

Lieberman, A. (1995). "Practices That Support Teacher Development." *Phi Delta Kappan* 76, 8: 591-596.

Little, J.W. (1993). "District Policy Choices and Teachers' Professional Development Opportunities." *Educational Evaluation and Policy Analysis* 11, 2: 165-179.

Louis Harris and Associates. (1995). *The Metropolitan Life Survey of the American Teacher, 1984-1995.* New York: Author.

McLaughlin, M.W. (1994). "Strategic Sites for Teachers' Professional Development." In *Teacher Development and the Struggle for Authenticity,* edited by P.P. Grimmett and J. Neufeld. New York: Teachers College Press, pp. 31-51.

Owens, R.G. (1987). "The Leadership of Educational Clans." In *Leadership: Examining the Elusive,* edited by L.T. Sheive and M.B. Schoenheit. Alexandria, Va.: Association for Supervision and Curriculum Development, pp. 16-29.

Schaefer, R.J. (1967). *The School as a Center of Inquiry.* New York: Harper and Row.

Sergiovanni, T.J. (1992). *Moral Leadership: Getting to the Heart of School Improvement.* San Francisco, Calif.: Jossey-Bass.

Smith, W.F., and R.L. Andrews. (1989). *Instructional Leadership: How Principals Make a Difference.* Alexandria, Va.: Association for Supervision and Curriculum Development.

3

Fostering the Learning-Centered Classroom

All the developmental services provided to teachers should foster the learning-centered classroom, which incorporates a focus on learning outcomes with an emphasis on a constructivist model of learning. The following discussion stresses the importance of an outcomes focus, explains the constructivist model, and then examines the implications for teacher development.

A Focus on Learning Outcomes

The learning-centered classroom focuses on the learning outcomes, not on the teacher's methods or the students' activities. These outcomes become central as the teacher plans, teaches, and reflects on the lesson. In too many instances, both experts and practitioners have focused on teaching methods, asking such questions as, "Did the teacher use an anticipatory set?" or "Did the teacher check for understanding?" The result is often classrooms where all the right methods have been used, but no significant learning has occurred.

Instead, in the learning-centered classroom, the focus is on learning outcomes. First, the plans for a given lesson come from the plans for the larger unit, to ensure a close fit between the unit and the individual lesson. In planning the specific lesson, the teacher first determines the outcomes for the lesson, ensuring that those outcomes meet the following criteria:

1. The lesson outcome is directly related to the unit goal or outcome.

2. The lesson outcome is significant: to that subject, for future learning, to the student, and for the unit.

3. The lesson outcome is developmentally appropriate, challenging but not out of reach.

The teacher plans to engage the student in the active construction of meaning. The teacher visualizes a sequence of meaningful learning tasks that will enable students to achieve the identified outcome. This visualization process is similar to the scenario for a film: The teacher sees in the mind's eye how the class activities unroll. The teacher reflects on how to assess student achievement of that outcome and tentatively identifies remediation strategies for those not achieving mastery.

Second, while teaching the lesson, the teacher focuses on the lesson outcome. At times, the teacher will make the outcome specific at the beginning of the lesson; at other times, the teacher will present the outcome in a general form to facilitate discovery. But students should not wonder where the lesson is headed. The teacher activates the planned scenario, monitoring in an ongoing manner and making modifications as needed. Throughout the lesson, the teacher reminds students of the outcome and points out how specific activities and tasks relate to the outcome. The teacher periodically assesses student progress and remediates as needed.

Finally, as the teacher reflects on the lesson in private or in a conference with a peer or supervisor, the teacher keeps the learning outcome central: Did all the students achieve the outcome? If so, what contributed? If not, what impeded? Thus, the bottom-line question is, "What did the students learn in that period that they did not know when they walked into the classroom?"

A Constructivist Approach to Learning

In recent years, a new view of learning has emerged—one with major implications for several aspects of schooling. This new perspective, called *constructivism*, emphasizes the learner as an active maker (or constructor) of meaning. This new view is an intrinsic and vital part of the learning-centered classroom. The teacher uses a constructivist perspective when identifying learning outcomes, developing the scenario for the lesson, and choosing assessment strategies.

The following discussion briefly examines the major principles of this constructivist approach to learning. (The discussion draws chiefly from the following sources: Brooks and Brooks 1993, Leinhardt 1992, Presidential Task Force on Psychology in Education 1993, and Rosenshine and Meister 1992.) Figure 3.1 (see p. 27) contrasts these principles with those of direct instruction.

Motivation Is Central to Learning.

Rather than seeing motivation as something separate from the learning process, cognitive psychologists emphasize the close interrelationship of motivation and cognition. Motivation has a significant cognitive component: Attitude about learning is influenced by perception of the nature of intelligence. And motivation affects cognition, both in wanting to acquire new learning and in deciding to apply what has been learned. If the learner does not apply newly acquired knowledge and skills, then what was learned is soon forgotten.

Learning Is Goal Oriented.

The learner focuses on meaningful goals—to engage with and master the environment, to construct meaning, and to make sense of the world. Thus, the student says, "I want to learn how to solve

Figure 3.1: Major Differences Between Direct Instruction and Constructivist Models

MODEL

Aspect	Direct Instruction	Constructivist
Research basis for model	Teacher effectiveness research	Cognitive psychology research
View of learning	Reception, retention	Active construction
Teacher's role	Transmitter, explainer	Scaffolder, one who structures problem solving
Discussion type	Recitation	Reflective dialogue
Nature of thinking	Isolated skills	Contextualized strategies
Nature of problems	Drill and practice	Meaningful, complex
View of errors	To be avoided	Natural; to be used
Most useful for teaching	Basic skills and concepts	Problem solving, critical thinking
Importance of content	Content not seen as essential	Content is essential; use generative content
Purposes of opening lesson segment	Review, develop anticipatory set	Activate prior knowledge
Purposes of middle lesson segment	Explain, demonstrate	Structure problem solving
Means of ensuring mastery	Guided, independent practice	Scaffolding

mathematical problems," not "I have to do those 10 examples." The emphasis is on the active processing of knowledge to apply it in meaningful ways.

Knowledge not applied is called inert knowledge, which lies dormant in the mind because either the learner cannot link it with prior knowledge or fails to gain access to it. (See Bransford, Sherwood, Vye, and Reiser 1986 for a fuller discussion of inert knowledge.) Knowledge applied and used to generate new knowledge is called generative knowledge.

Learning is the active construction of meaning, not a passive receptive process. Learning is the ability to perform complex cognitive tasks that require use and application of knowledge. Learning involves conceptual change—modifying one's previous understanding of concepts so they are more complex and valid. In this sense, learning is always subjective and personal. People learn best when they can internalize what is learned and represent it through learner-generated symbols, metaphors, graphics, and models.

Learning requires gaining new knowledge and relating that new knowledge to prior knowledge. As Resnick and Klopfer (1989) emphasize, experts reason more effectively in areas where they have a deep knowledge base. Chess masters know chess patterns and moves so thoroughly they can quickly make sound predictions and brilliant moves; but they do not reason effectively in other areas of life where their expertise is limited.

The learner's knowledge base is always growing. The learner challenges what is already known, analyzes new information in relation to existing knowledge, and integrates the old and the new into modified knowledge structures.

Subject matter content, problem-solving, and thinking skills are closely interrelated. Rather than accept the content/skill dichotomy, cognitive psychologists see them as closely intertwined. Students can reason about the causes of the Civil War only if they have extensive knowledge about society's conditions prior to the war. In this sense, this principle is a corollary of the preceding one and also serves as a reminder that the construction of knowledge best occurs when the learner deals with meaningful problems that must be solved. Rather than learning isolated "thinking skills," the learner engages in solving meaningful problems that require generative knowledge and certain problem-solving strategies. This type of activity results in contextualized knowledge—knowledge that is understood in the context of challenging tasks.

Knowledge is best acquired, retained, and used when organized in meaningful ways. As Jones and her colleagues (1988) note, experts have better organized knowledge structures than do novices. Rather than acquiring unrelated pieces of information, experts use organizing systems to help them store knowledge more efficiently and to access it more readily. Thus, if you ask lay people to identify the types of workers in schools, they will randomly list them: "Let's see—there's a principal, many teachers, teacher aides, some cafeteria workers." The experienced professional has them organized mentally and accesses them this way: "PROFESSIONALS: school administrators, classroom teachers, other professionals; NONPROFESSIONALS: secretaries, custodians, aides, and other nonprofessional support staff."

Learning involves developing and using cognitive and metacognitive strategies. These strategies are mental operations and structures that simplify and increase the effectiveness of learning. Some strategies, such as identifying the essential elements of a narrative, are domain- or subject-specific; others, such as activating prior knowledge, are more generic. The learner knows how and when to use those strategies and makes effective use of them when appropriate. Because of the significance of these strategies, the constructivist model is sometimes called strategic teaching.

Learning occurs best through apprenticeships in social settings. Two elements of this principle need to be noted. The first is the concept of cognitive apprenticeships. As Resnick and Klopfer (1989) explain, cognitive apprenticeships apply the significant features of traditional craft apprenticeships to the work of learning. The apprenticeship requires a real task, rather than a contrived exercise, and is built upon the contextualized practice of tasks, not isolated drills. Finally, learning apprenticeships provide opportunities for learners to observe others doing the kind of intellectual work the learners are expected to do.

Resnick (1987) also observes that the most successful programs for teaching higher-order cognitive skills embed learning in a social context: Students work together on problems and observe and help each other master the new skill. If students can become active members of learning communities, they will become more inclined to value learning and appreciate its power.

Scaffolding helps in the problem-solving process. Scaffolding is a metaphor for cognitive structure. At the initial stages of the learning process, the learner functions best with high structure, using teacher-provided cues, specific explanations, and organizing strategies to make sense of the problem and engage in its solution. As the learner progresses, less scaffolding is needed; the goal is to turn over the entire process to the learner so the learner becomes self-regulating. (See Rosenshine and Meister 1992 for the use of scaffolding in teaching specific strategies.)

The Implications for Teachers' Professional Development

Obviously, the learning-centered classroom has implications for fostering teachers' growth that can be summed up under the rubric of learning-centered development, a developmental process that focuses on learning outcomes. Unlike most standard versions of clinical supervision that focus on teaching methods, learning-centered development focuses on what is learned. The following discussion examines the specific implications of the model for the observation/conference process and then considers the implications of the learning-centered classroom for other developmental functions.

Learning-Centered Observations and Conferences

Here, briefly, is the process a learning-centered supervisor would use in carrying out learning-centered development (the term supervisor is used in the following discussion to refer to any professional who observes and gives feedback):

• **The Pre-Observation Conference.** In the pre-observation conference (if one is held), the supervisor would focus on these related issues (which are introduced by questions):

1. What are the intended learning outcomes? In examining this issue, the supervisor should be chiefly concerned with these matters. Are the outcomes clear in the teacher's mind? Are the lesson outcomes related to the unit outcomes? Are the lesson outcomes significant? Are the outcomes developmentally appropriate?

2. What work will the students do to achieve those outcomes? The emphasis is on student productivity and the quality of the learning experience. Do the tasks actively involve the students in the construction of meaning? Are the students engaged in meaningful learning? In too many classes, the teacher does all the work, while the students sit passively—or the teacher provides meaningless "drills" that require little active processing.

3. What methods will the teacher use to assess learning? The teacher must be aware of the importance of ongoing assessment.

4. Does the teacher's view of the lesson suggest that the teacher understands and can apply a constructivist view of learning?

The supervisor makes clear to the teacher that the observation and the postobservation conference will deal with these issues.

• **The Classroom Observation.** The supervisor focuses on observing to answer these questions:

1. How would you describe the learning outcome and its significance? Was it significant to the unit studied; significant in relation to the key ideas and skills of that subject; significant to the learner; and significant to future learning?

2. How many students seem to have mastered the objective or outcome? What did they know when the period ended that they did not know when the period began? What is the evidence that learning occurred?

3. What work were the students engaged in, and what was the quality? Who did most of the work? How many students were meaningfully engaged? What was the quality of the learning experience?

4. How did the teacher assess learning? How often did assessment occur? How many students were involved?

Perhaps the best method for recording observations is "script taping," making a complete record of all important transactions. The questions listed in Figure 3.2 (see p. 32) should help anyone observing a lesson from a learning perspective. Remember that these questions should not be used as a prescriptive checklist to evaluate teaching.

**Figure 3.2: Questions to Ask While Observing
a Learning-Centered Classroom***

---

1. Did the teacher seem sensitive to the importance of intrinsic motivation by helping students find meaning and purpose in what was to be learned?

2. Was the learning objective significant and clear to all? Did the teacher help the students internalize the objective as a learning goal?

3. Did the teacher help students activate prior knowledge?

4. Did the teacher help students gain access to new knowledge, and were the means of access and the source of knowledge the most efficient and effective?

5. Did the teacher help students relate the new knowledge to prior knowledge and modify knowledge constructs accordingly?

6. Did the teacher help students construct personal meaning by having them organize, elaborate, and represent knowledge in their own way?

7. Did the teacher help students identify a complex problem that requires them to apply generative knowledge?

8. Did the teacher provide an appropriate amount of scaffolding to enable the students to solve the problem?

9. Did the teacher teach the strategies needed to solve the problem?

10. Did the teacher provide a supportive social context with reflective dialogue and cooperative inquiry?

11. Did the teacher help the students use metacognitive monitoring to assess their learning?

12. Did the teacher make periodic assessments of learning and use assessment data to adjust and remediate?

* The questions are intended to guide observation and do not represent a prescriptive checklist.

• **The Observational Analysis.** Now the supervisor examines the record and reflects on the identified issues. If significant learning took place for all the students, how is that explained? If such learning did not take place, how is that explained? At this stage, the supervisor may wish to focus on teaching methods, which are ancillary issues to raise in an explanatory mode and not the focus of the analysis.

• **The Postobservation Conference.** In the postobservation conference, the supervisor poses the following questions to the teacher:

1. From your perception, was the learning objective clear and significant? What evidence can you provide?

2. What percentage of the students have mastered the objective? What evidence can you provide?

3. What work did the students do to achieve the objective, and did that work add up to a quality learning experience? To what extent were the students actively involved in the construction of meaning? What evidence can you provide?

4. How do you explain the students' success or seeming lack of success?

5. What are the implications of this lesson for our work together?

The intent is to help teachers become reflective about teaching relative to student learning. The supervisor uses a problem-solving mode to foster such reflection.

The Implications for Other Developmental Services

The hope is that the principles of the learning-centered classroom permeate all the developmental services provided to teachers. Staff development programs should ensure that all teachers understand and can apply the basic principles of constructivism to their classes. The informal observations by the principal should focus on learning. And teachers working in both the cooperative and the self-directed modes should emphasize mastery of constructivist approaches in their own professional development.

References

Bransford, J.D., R. Sherwood, N. Vye, and J. Reiser. (1986). "Teaching Thinking and Problem Solving." *American Psychologist* 41, pp. 1078–1089.

Brooks, J.G., and M.G. Brooks. (1993). *In Search of Understanding: The Case for Constructivist Classrooms.* Alexandria, Va.: Association for Supervision and Curriculum Development.

Jones, B.F., A. Palincsar, D.S. Ogle, and E.G. Carr. (1988). *Strategic Thinking and Learning: Cognitive Instruction in the Content Areas.* Alexandria, Va.: Association for Supervision and Curriculum Development.

Leinhardt, G. (April 1992). "What Research on Learning Tells Us About Teaching." *Educational Leadership* 49 ,7: 20-25.

Presidential Task Force on Psychology in Education, American Psychological Association. (1993). *Learner-Centered Psychological Principles: Guidelines for School Redesign and Reform.* Washington, D.C.: Author.

Resnick, L.B. (1987). *Education and Learning to Think.* Washington, D.C.: National Academy Press.

Resnick, L.B., and L.E. Klopfer. (1989). "Toward the Thinking Curriculum: An Overview." In *Toward the Thinking Curriculum: Current Cognitive Research,* edited by L.B. Resnick and L.E. Klopfer. Alexandria, Va.: Association for Supervision and Curriculum Development, pp. 1-20.

Rosenshine, B., and C. Meister. (April 1992). "The Use of Scaffolds for Teaching Higher-Level Cognitive Strategies." *Educational Leadership* 49, 7: 26-33.

The Developmental Options of Differentiated Supervision

4

Providing Intensive Development

As explained in Chapter 1, intensive development is a special form of "clinical supervision" usually provided to two groups of teachers: all nontenured teachers, and all tenured teachers experiencing serious problems. As emphasized in the preceding chapter, educators using intensive development are encouraged to base it on the principles of the learning-centered classroom.

The following discussion clarifies the differences between standard clinical supervision and the intensive development model recommended here and then offers a detailed explanation of how the model operates. The critique of clinical supervision that follows is concerned with the weaknesses of clinical supervision as usually applied by busy supervisors, and not with the clinical supervision as recommended by experts.

Differences Between the Two Models

Significant differences exist between the standard form of clinical supervision and the intensive development model that plays a part in differentiated supervision.

First, clinical supervision is usually concerned with teaching methods; intensive development, with learning outcomes. Clinical supervision is provided to all teachers in most of its models; intensive development is offered only to those who need it. Because clinical supervision is offered to the entire faculty, the standard model has superficial impact: On the average, teachers are observed only twice a year. (See Badiali and Levin 1984.) On the other hand, intensive development typically involves five or more cycles of the supervisory process, with multiple observations, because only a small group of teachers is involved. Finally, the standard model of clinical supervision relies on one type of observation followed by analysis and conference. Intensive development, as explained below, draws from a more varied set of tools.

Using Intensive Development

The following discussion identifies some special features of intensive development; presents an overview of its several components; then explains how each component functions, including an example of how a supervisor would use them with a new teacher.

Special Features of Intensive Development

Three features should be stressed at the outset. First, intensive development is concerned solely with teacher growth and is divorced from teacher evaluation. The details of the developmental process should not be shared with the principal, unless the teacher authorizes such sharing. This firm wall between development and evaluation is essential. Growth requires an open relationship, and openness and evaluation are essentially incompatible.

Second, if development and evaluation are separated, the person responsible for evaluation should not provide the intensive development. Depending on the size of the school and the personnel resources available, one of the following can be responsible for the intensive development: a central office supervisor, an administrator who does not have an evaluation responsibility, a department chair, a team leader, or a colleague-mentor.

Finally, the relationship should be permeated with a sense of collaborative inquiry. Rather than the supervisor behaving like an expert with all the answers, the supervisor works collaboratively with the teacher in a spirit of inquiry and reflection. Sometimes the supervisor will draw upon experience, but most often the supervisor will foster reflection on the part of the teacher.

The Components of Intensive Development

The model's comprehensive version includes eight components:*

1. Taking-stock conference. A conference held at the start of the year, at the end of the year, or any time in between when the supervisor and the teacher sense a need to reflect on what has been accomplished and where the relationship is headed. It may subsume some of the functions of the pre-observation conference.

2. Pre-observation conference. An optional conference to review the teacher's plans for the lesson to be observed and to determine the purpose of the observation.

3. Diagnostic observation. An observation of teaching to collect full data about all relevant aspects of learning and teaching for the purpose of diagnosing the teacher's needs.

4. Analysis of diagnostic observation. An analysis by the supervisor and the teacher, either individually or together, of the diagnostic observational data to determine a focus for the developmental work.

5. Diagnostic debriefing conference. A conference between the supervisor and the teacher to analyze the lesson and to reflect on its importance for development.

6. Coaching session. A meeting that provides coaching for a specific skill identified through the diagnostic process. Coaching usually includes the following: providing a knowledge base for the skill; explaining the skill; demonstrating the skill; providing for guided practice, with feedback; and providing for independent practice, with feedback.

---

* The term supervisor denotes any professional providing these services, including a central office supervisor, a school administrator, a team leader, and a mentor.

7. Focused observation. An observation that focuses on one skill, using a form designed to collect information about the teacher's use of that skill.

8. Focused debriefing conference. A debriefing conference that reviews and analyzes the results of the focused observation.

How the Model Operates

The following discussion explains how these eight components work together to help a novice teacher improve skills. Each component is explained fully. An example is then provided showing how Sue Noblit, middle school team leader, would use that component to serve the developmental needs of Bill Olsen, a first-year teacher on Sue's team.

Taking-Stock Conferences

The taking-stock conference is an informal discussion to make a formative assessment of the developmental relationship. Taking-stock conferences should always occur at the beginning and at the end of the year. They can also occur throughout the year to assess progress and make plans.

The first purpose of the initial taking-stock conference usually deals with three general issues: the supervisory contract, the context for teaching, and the beliefs of the supervisor and teacher. In clarifying the supervisory contract, the supervisor and the teacher should discuss the following issues:

1. The primary purpose of the relationship—developmental or evaluative.

2. The nature of supervisory observations—their focus, number, frequency, and type. The supervisor and teacher also discuss the means used to record and store observational data, such as written notes, audiotapes, videotapes, and computer records.

3. The nature of supervisory conferences—their type, purpose, and frequency.

4. The record-keeping process—the kinds of records and notes that will be made, if those notes become part of the official record, and if the teacher has access to them.

5. Other available supervisory services and resources—the people and materials that can assist growth.

The second general purpose of this initial conference is to clarify the teaching context. The supervisor and teacher examine such issues as community values, the district and school cultures, the teacher's schedule, the nature of the students, the curriculum, and any other elements of the context that will affect teaching.

Finally, the initial conference provides an opportunity for the supervisor and teacher to discuss their belief systems. As Richardson (1990) notes, the teacher's belief system has a strong influence on how the teacher performs in the classroom. Ordinarily, the following issues are examined: the role of the schools, the role of the teacher, preferred models of teaching, the ethical dimension of teaching and supervising, the teacher's role in curriculum development, and attitudes toward students and classroom environment. Through open dialogue, the supervisor discerns the teacher's practical knowledge about classroom life and about teaching and learning practices.

One or two taking-stock conferences are held throughout the year, depending upon need and time available. These midyear conferences have two related purposes: to look back and to look ahead. In looking back, the supervisor and teacher assess the nature and extent of the teacher's growth and how the supervisory process has or has not facilitated that growth. In looking ahead, the two plan a tentative agenda for the next phase of their work together.

The end-of-year taking-stock conference is chiefly concerned with reflecting on the past year and identifying some tentative growth goals for the coming year. Note that this reflective analysis is concerned with the growth of both the teacher and the supervisor.

Sue Noblit, the 7th grade team leader, holds the initial taking-stock conference during the inservice days prior to the opening of the school year. She explains to Bill Olsen, the new teacher, that her work with him will be solely developmental, with no evaluation implied. She reviews the components of the developmental cycle, indicating that she likes to apply it flexibly. She plans to wait a few weeks before making the first diagnostic observation to give Bill time to get settled. She also explains that she prefers to observe two related lessons in the same unit before holding a debriefing conference, which enables her to see connections between lessons and get a more reliable picture of the teacher's performance. Bill strongly approves of this approach.

Sue gives Bill some basic information about the community and the district, and they review Bill's schedule and his students.

When Sue and Bill discuss their belief systems, Sue lets Bill take the initiative, so as not to bias his presentation. Bill indicates that he firmly believes in making extensive use of cooperative learning, with students monitoring their own performance. When queried by Sue, Bill reports that he had only a brief introduction to constructivist learning in his methods course and is still unsure how to use it. Sue reassures him that he will have opportunities to learn more about it and to observe teachers skilled in using it.

Sue notes that she likes using cooperative learning, but introduces it only after a few weeks of teacher-directed learning; she also points out that she has very strict accountability procedures for students' cooperative work.

Pre-Observation Conferences

The chief purpose of the pre-observation conference is to make the observation more productive by enabling the supervisor and the teacher to set the stage for the observation. As noted in the previous chapter, the conference enables the supervisor and the teacher to consider the following learning-related issues:

• **The Intended Learning Outcomes.** Are they clear in the teacher's mind? Are they related to a unit, which in turn is derived from the approved curriculum? Are the outcomes significant and developmentally appropriate?

• **The Students' Work.** What tasks will students perform to accomplish the outcomes? Are tasks meaningful, engaging students in the construction of meaning?

42

• **The Means of Assessment.** How will learning be assessed? To what extent are the methods authentic? How will the teacher use assessment data to modify instruction?

• **The Overall Nature of the Lesson.** Will it likely result in significant learning? Does it reflect the principles of constructivism?

What should be the tone and style of these and other conferences? Some research suggests that most novices and some experienced teachers with low cognitive maturity prefer a more direct style. (See, for example, Copeland 1980, Glickman 1985.) In using the direct style, the supervisor tells, demonstrates, and advises. However, the research also indicates that most experienced teachers prefer a problem-solving style that uses reflective dialogue, with the supervisor asking probing questions that help the teacher think critically about teaching and learning. (See Copeland 1982, Konke 1984.) On the whole, a flexible approach seems to make more sense. The supervisor and the teacher openly discuss this matter of style, and the supervisor intentionally uses elements of both styles. The general goal is to move the teacher toward growth-independence and self-analytical thinking.

The first pre-observation conference can be part of the initial taking-stock conference. Succeeding conferences can be scheduled flexibly, depending upon the preferences of both the supervisor and the teacher. If time is limited and if the relationship has been developing in a productive manner, the pre-observation conference can be omitted.

Sue schedules a pre-observation conference with Bill during the last week of September. Bill asks Sue to observe his second period social studies class. Bill has modified another teacher's unit on Mexico and would appreciate Sue's feedback about his teaching.

Sue says that she would like to observe two lessons, one taught early in the unit and one later. When Sue asks Bill about the intended learning outcomes for the first lesson, he identifies this one: Explain how the geography of Mexico affects people. Sue asks if the objective might be too general. After some open discussion, Bill modifies it this way: Explain how the geography of Mexico affects how Mexicans earn their living. In further discussion of learning activities and assessment strategies, Sue is satisfied that Bill has planned an interesting lesson. She is still concerned that Bill is too activity oriented, but she decides not to pursue the issue because Bill is showing some early signs of defensiveness.

Diagnostic Observations

Diagnostic observations collect all meaningful interactions so the supervisor and teacher can determine the teacher's strengths and developmental needs. The supervisor scans the classroom with a learning focus, remembering the four questions noted in Chapter 3: (1) What is the learning outcome and how significant is it? (2) How many students seem to have achieved the outcome? (3) What work are the students engaged in and what is the quality? and (4) How is learning being assessed?

Some supervisors prefer to record their observations on a blank pad, and some prefer the computer or video. A simple form (see Figure 4.1) may facilitate recording observational data. Forms, though, should be open-ended. Forms listing evaluative criteria or including a checklist of expected behaviors are too structured for the purposes of diagnosis.

Figure 4.1: Sample Form for Diagnostic Observation

Date and Time	Learner Actions	Teacher Actions
Sept. 26, 1996 10:15 a.m.	Working individually on text questions, five students seem off task.	Sitting at desk

The following guidelines for the observer making diagnostic observations come from the literature and this author's experience:

1. If possible, observe the first, middle, and last lessons in a unit. Teachers want observers to see a sequence, not one lesson out of context.

2. Arrive at the beginning of the lesson and stay until the end. The opening and closing of the session are crucial periods, and the supervisor should be present.

3. Sit where you can see the faces of the teacher and most of the students, because body language is a vital element of communication.

4. Minimize the intrusive aspects of the observation. Take a seat quietly, avoid getting involved with students, and interrupt the teacher only in a dire emergency.

5. Be sure to record the time of all significant interactions, because time is an important element in learning.

6. Scan the entire classroom, rather than focusing solely on the teacher. Remember that the key issue is student learning.

7. Suspend judgment. Experienced observers tend to make mental evaluations as they observe, such as: "Why can't he see that the students are bored?" Impulsive judgments, however, should be held in check.

8. Make the notes as objective and as specific as possible. For example: "Five students playing with objects on their desks; three are exchanging comments with each other; one student has his head on the desk."

9. Use verbatim quotes for words that seem to have an impact or reveal feelings. A quote, such as this, says more than a paraphrase:

"I don't expect you to know this for the test, but it is important, especially for Billy here who just might sneak into college."

10. Focus on the key elements of learning and teaching. Avoid less vital information, such as the quality of bulletin boards, the teacher's appearance or dress, and the teacher's voice—unless these clearly affect learning.

11. Because observational notes will often be shared with the teacher, remember that they may become a public document. Be legible, accurate, and professional.

12. Put yourself in the teacher's shoes. Understand the lesson from the teacher's perspective. Assume that the teacher is rational, professional, and wants to teach effectively.

13. As you observe, remember that classrooms are complex environments affected by the organizational culture, the professional support system, the students, and the teacher. Do not assume that classroom problems are solely the result of teacher errors.

Sue uses the form shown in Figure 4.1 to record her observations. She keeps a time-structured record, notes evidence of the extent of student learning, and strives for objectivity, even though she feels uncomfortable about what she sees as unstructured group work.

Analysis of Diagnostic Observations

The supervisor now analyzes the observational data. In most cases, the supervisor should involve the teacher in a collaborative analysis, which is especially useful if a video record of the class is available.

The analysis should tentatively identify nonteacher factors that might have influenced the classroom performance and the teacher's strengths that can be built upon, as well as assess the teacher's needs that should become the focus of the developmental process.

To accomplish these purposes, the supervisor (working alone or with the teacher) should first consider the lesson in its totality, before adopting an analytical stance. The supervisor asks these two general questions:

"Did significant learning take place for most of the students?"

"What factors, other than teacher factors, might have affected the learning?"

This holistic assessment enables the supervisor to determine if school culture, students' behavior, or elements of the instructional support system might be modified.

The supervisor's attention should turn next to the teacher's actions, attempting to link them diagnostically to student learning. The supervisor should again review the entire observational record to determine critical points in the lesson where learning seemed maximized. Such points would exhibit the following characteristics: Students demonstrate a high level of on-task behavior, students demonstrate strong motivation to learn, and student responses indicate that significant learning is taking place. The supervisor then analyzes which teacher behaviors helped to facilitate this high level of learning. This analysis of the maximizing of learning enables the supervisor to identify strengths that should be affirmed in the debriefing conference.

The supervisor next reviews the entire record a second time to determine critical points where learning seemed minimized, searching for evidence of this sort: Students seemed inattentive and off task; and students' responses suggested they were confused, misinformed, or lacked sufficient knowledge. The supervisor then looks for the teacher behaviors that might have been responsible for minimizing learning.

The teacher factors that ordinarily result in minimizing learning are shown in Figure 4.2 (see p. 48).

To structure this analysis, the supervisor might use a form like the one shown in Figure 4.3 (see p. 49). It serves as a reminder of the key issues that require examination.

Again, this analysis can occur in two ways: The supervisor can perform it alone, identifying a tentative agenda for the debriefing conference and using that tentative agenda to structure the debriefing conference; or the supervisor and teacher can do it collaboratively at the debriefing conference.

Sue observes the second lesson scheduled for analysis and decides to analyze the lessons first on her own and then collaboratively with Bill. Her analysis of these two lessons leads her to certain tentative conclusions. First, she did not see sufficient evidence of significant learning in either lesson. Sue realizes that the school culture has not yet had an impact. She taught these students before and knows that several of them have weak motivation to learn and that they see the classroom as a place to have fun. As Sue examines the instructional support system, she realizes the textbook contains inadequate treatment of the topic.

Sue then focuses on those places in the lesson where student learning seemed maximized. In reviewing her notes, she remembers that she was impressed with Bill's ability to help students activate their knowledge of Mexico by writing what they already knew, listing the information on the board, and then identifying what questions they would like answered.

Figure 4.2: Teacher Instructional Errors

Teacher Motivation

1. The teacher does not convey a high degree of professional motivation and enthusiasm.

Teacher Knowledge

2. The teacher does not exhibit sufficient knowledge of the subject and the students.

Teacher Planning

3. The teacher does not seem to have made effective plans for learning and has not made adequate preparation for the lesson.

Teacher Skills

4. The teacher has not tried to make the lesson meaningful and motivational.

5. The teacher does not help students access prior knowledge and determine its accuracy and comprehensiveness.

6. The teacher has not clarified the objective or has identified an objective that is not developmentally appropriate.

7. The teacher does not seem able to sustain an orderly and supportive learning environment.

8. The teacher does not provide sufficient scaffolding or structure.

9. The teacher does not provide an appropriate pace of learning and does not make effective use of time.

10. The teacher does not monitor student learning.

11. The teacher provides learning activities unlikely to achieve the objective.

12. The teacher does not provide sufficient variety in the learning tasks.

13. The teacher does not help students achieve valid and personal understandings of the lesson and make connections with their own lives.

Sue also identifies several places in both lessons where learning seemed minimized. Bill seemed unskilled in monitoring student learning, especially when students worked together in small groups. And most of the small-group discussions did not seem grounded in a solid knowledge base: Students were guessing and arguing instead of using knowledge sources.

Figure 4.3: Form for Analyzing Diagnostic Observation

---

1. **Lesson Objective**: _____ —

2. **Student Achievement.** To what extent did most of the students achieve significant learning?

3. **Nonteacher Factors.** What factors (other than teacher factors) might have affected student learning?

4. **Learning Maximized**
   - At which points in the lesson did learning seem maximized?
   - Which teacher behaviors might have contributed?

5. **Learning Minimized**
   - At which points in the lesson did learning seem minimized?
   - Which teacher behaviors might have contributed?

Diagnostic Debriefing Conference

The diagnostic debriefing conference should clearly show the hallmarks of collaborative inquiry:

- **Data-Rich.** The conference is based on objective data, with both parties minimizing subjective evaluations.
- **Mutual and Cooperative.** The conference is conducted in a manner that respects the knowledge and the perspectives of both the teacher and the supervisor. They work together as colleagues to solve significant teaching and learning problems.
- **Problem Solving and Reflective.** The conference attempts to solve learning problems, not to evaluate or criticize. The supervisor is concerned with helping the teacher examine beliefs and knowledge, especially as they affected performance.
- **Productive.** The conference emphasizes teacher strengths and how those strengths can be the foundation for future work. The conference moves to solutions.

With copies of the observational record in their hands, the supervisor and the teacher work through the analysis process. In general, the supervisor should ask questions that structure the analysis, using the sequence shown in Figure 4.2. The supervisor must understand how to respond to the teacher's statements, using the following responses appropriately:

Agree: I agree with you about that. I have reached the same conclusion. Those are the concerns I feel.

Disagree: I have different data. The observations seem to suggest another interpretation.

Probe: Can you point to where that occurred? Why do you believe that? Where is the evidence for that conclusion?

Reflect: Why do you think that happened? What might have caused that?

Paraphrase: You seem to be blaming the students—am I right? You think you were chiefly at fault, is that the case?

The goal of the conference is to help the teacher become more insightful and reflective by using this problem-solving orientation. If the teacher seems to have difficulty in solving instructional problems, then the supervisor may need to provide more scaffolding, just as a teacher provides scaffolding for students. Here is an example of the supervisor providing scaffolding:

"I know it's difficult at times to figure out what was going on. Try putting yourself in the students' shoes. It's Friday afternoon. It has been a long day. The teacher is talking about the amoeba. What are you thinking about?"

Bill begins the analysis by indicating that he thinks the lessons were generally successful. When Sue asks him for the evidence supporting that conclusion, he seems nonplussed. Sue indicates they can maintain their differing judgments until they have examined the lessons in more detail. Sue next focuses Bill's attention on the way he helped students activate prior knowledge. Her questions are designed to help him understand and then validate this strength.

50

Bill has difficulty identifying critical points in the lessons where learning seemed minimized. Sue uses that opening to raise the issue of monitoring student learning, especially when students work in small groups. Bill acknowledges that he is unsure how to accomplish this goal without being too intrusive. They agree that it would be a good skill to develop and make plans to develop that skill.

Sue then directs Bill's attention to several places in the lesson where students seemed off task or confused. Bill seems to be getting defensive, and Sue decides not to press the issue. They conclude the conference by agreeing to do some coaching on the skill of monitoring small-group learning and deciding on a day and time for the coaching session.

Coaching Sessions

Coaching is often equated with the peer-coaching model developed and disseminated by Joyce and Showers (1983), who link it with staff development and models of teaching. In this book, coaching is used in a narrower sense than that used in the Joyce and Showers' book to refer to systematic training provided to a teacher to help that teacher acquire a teaching skill. Confusion about terminology may be the reason that the research on coaching is somewhat inconclusive. Showers, Joyce, and Bennett (1987) conclude from their review of four studies that virtually all the teachers involved reached the desired skill level. However, Wade's (1985) review of 225 cases of coaching yielded no evidence that coaching enhances instructional effectiveness. If coaching refers to systematic training, then its effectiveness depends upon the quality of that systematic training, which usually involves several related steps:

1. Develop the knowledge base. The supervisor provides some basic information about the skill to be developed: what the skill is; why the skill is important; what steps are involved; when the skill is best used; what problems to expect in using the skill; what research supports the use of the skill; and what resources are available. All this information can be summarized in what this author calls a "coaching protocol," which is a packet of information the teacher can read in preparing for

the session. These coaching protocols can be kept on file for easy use. (A set of protocols on the basic skills of teaching can be found in Glatthorn 1990.)

2. Demonstrate the skill. After reviewing the information in the coaching protocol, the supervisor demonstrates the skill or shows a videotape demonstrating the skill. The teacher should be invited to give the supervisor feedback about the demonstration.

3. Facilitate guided practice of the skill. Now the teacher has a chance to demonstrate the skill. This guided practice should occur in an emotionally safe environment—the teacher's vacant classroom, the supervisor's office, or a private conference room. The supervisor supports and encourages the teacher in the guided practice, but offers the necessary corrective feedback.

4. Plan for independent practice. When the guided practice is concluded, the supervisor and the teacher plan for the teacher's independent practice of the skill, with feedback. The teacher chooses a time to use the skill. Teacher and supervisor then develop or adapt a form the supervisor will use in conducting a focused observation, as explained below.

Remember, this coaching session has focused on one skill that the diagnostic observation and analysis have identified as needing development.

Focused Observation

A focused observation usually follows the coaching session within a few days. As the term implies, this observation examines only one facet of the teaching/learning process and in most instances will be the skill singled out for coaching and further development. In some cases, the focused observation can examine a skill introduced in a staff development program. Focused observation can be a powerful tool for development any time a teacher wants feedback on one specific aspect of teaching and learning.

Once the focus is determined collaboratively, the supervisor and the teacher select, adapt, or develop a focused observation form. This form is a structured instrument that facilitates the observation and recording processes. Several types of forms are available:

• *Seating charts* show the name of each student and the location of each student's desk, with space available for recording a coded entry. Seating charts are essential when the focus of the observation requires information about specific students. For example, if the skill is keeping students on task, a seating chart would show which students are on task and which are off task.

• *Checklists* are lists of specific behaviors that relate to a particular skill. For example, a checklist on monitoring student learning in small groups might include this list of skills:

1. Trains student leaders to monitor.
2. Establishes and performs a student accountability system.
3. Closely observes nonverbal behaviors in groups.
4. Monitors students' oral responses.
5. Requires students to demonstrate their learning at end of small-group session.
6. Questions students to assess small-group learning.

Checklists are useful when the skill observed involves several related subskills.

• *Time and quantity records* are forms that provide space for the observer to note the time a particular behavior occurs and the number of students involved in that behavior. These forms are especially useful for noting patterns of student attention over the course of the instructional session.

• *Exchange lists* are several kinds of forms developed by Good and Brophy (1991) and others, which enable the observer to collect two types of related information. The exchange list is usually a chart that lists down the left-hand side selected teacher or student behaviors and then shows across the top the specific categories of information desired. For example, if the observer wanted data on how the teacher responds to student answers, the form might list down the left the types of student answers (such as "correct," "incorrect," "vague or uncertain," "multiple," and "no answer") and across the top, the types of teacher responses (such as "praise," "negate," "paraphrase," "probe," and "use"). Such a matrix enables the observer to show the relationships of data. Several excellent forms are available in Good and Brophy (1991).

When the focus has been mutually identified and the form developed, the supervisor then observes the class and records information. The focused observation should be brief because the data collection process is so intense; Good and Brophy recommend a 15-minute limit.

Focused Debriefing Conference

The focused debriefing conference is easy for both the supervisor and the teacher. They review the data shown on the form and make their own sense of it, looking for patterns of behavior, as in this example:

After five minutes, about 90 percent of the class seemed on task. In the central part of the lesson when the teacher was explaining, on-task rates ranged from 50 percent to 75 percent. During the quiz that ended the lesson, on-task behavior raised to almost 100 percent.

At the end of the debriefing conference, the supervisor and the teacher can decide what next step should be taken: another coaching session on the same skill, another focused observation on the same skill, or another diagnostic observation.

Concluding Note

Obviously, intensive development as presented here is a complex and time-consuming process that goes far beyond the standard two observations and two conferences. However, under the differentiated system, intensive development is for that small group of teachers who need it.

References

Badiali, B., and J. Levin. (April 1984). "Supervisors' Responses to the Survey." Paper presented at annual meeting of the American Educational Research Association, New Orleans. (ERIC Document Reproduction Service No. 259 486).

Copeland, W.D. (1980). "Affective Dispositions of Teachers in Training Toward Examples of Supervisory Behavior." *Journal of Teacher Education* 74, pp. 37–42.

Copeland, W.D. (1982). "Student Teachers' Preferences for Supervisory Approach." *Journal of Teacher Education* 33, pp. 32–36.

Glatthorn, A.A. (1990). *Supervisory Leadership.* New York: HarperCollins.

Glickman, C.D. (1985). *Supervision of Instruction: A Developmental Approach.* Newton, Mass.: Allyn and Bacon.

Good, T.L., and J.E. Brophy. (1991). *Looking in Classrooms.* 5th ed. New York: HarperCollins.

Joyce, B.R., and B. Showers. (1983). *Power in Staff Development Through Research on Training.* Alexandria, Va.: Association for Supervision and Curriculum Development.

Konke, K. (1984). "A Study of the Relationship of Teachers' Conceptual Level with Perceptions of Teachers in Regard to Staff Development, Curriculum Development, and Instructional Improvement." Paper presented at annual meeting of the American Educational Research Association, New Orleans.

Richardson, V. (1990). "Significant and Worthwhile Change in Teaching Practice." *Educational Researcher* 19, 7: 10–18.

Showers, B., B. Joyce, and B. Bennett. (1987). "Synthesis of Research on Staff Development: A Framework for Future Study and a State-of-the-Art Analysis." *Educational Leadership* 43, 3: 77–87.

Wade, R.K. (1985). "What Makes a Difference in Inservice Teacher Education? A Meta-Analysis of Research." *Educational Leadership* 42, 4: 48–54.

5

Fostering Cooperative Professional Development

Cooperative professional development is one of the options provided in the differentiated model. In this book, the term is defined as

A process of fostering teachers' development through systematic peer collaboration.

This chapter accomplishes several related goals: presenting a rationale for this component, explaining the forms it takes, describing the operation of a typical program, and reviewing the necessary steps to ensure its success.

A Rationale for Cooperative Professional Development

Cooperative professional development can be justified from several perspectives. From the perspective of the organization, it systematically harnesses teachers' time and energy for the improvement of the school. Although individual teacher efforts are needed for school improvement, collaborative work that capitalizes on teachers' skills is more likely to make an impact. (See Smith and Scott 1990.) Also, cooperative professional development strengthens the linkages between school improvement and teacher growth. In the cooperative model, teacher development is not seen as an end unto itself but as a powerful method for improving learning through better teaching.

From the supervisor's perspective (including district supervisors and school administrators), cooperative professional development enables the supervisor to affect a larger number of teachers, rather than working with one teacher at a time. Although cooperative professional development is essentially managed and directed by teachers, the supervisor can provide a vital supportive role by securing resources, providing needed expertise, and working with the group to solve problems.

The cooperative model has several advantages from the teacher's perspective: It recognizes and rewards the professionalism of teachers and empowers them to take charge of their own development; it reduces the isolation of teachers, enabling them to interact with colleagues about professional issues; it opens the classroom door to new ideas, to collegial sources of help, and to input from concerned colleagues; and it responds to teachers' preference for colleagues as a source of assistance. Zahorik (1987) discovered that teachers receive from each other 11 kinds of help: materials, discipline, learning activities, individualization, student evaluation, methods, objectives, reinforcing students, lecturing, questioning, and room organization.

This rationale is not to suggest, of course, that cooperative professional development is without its problems. As explained later in this chapter, it has its own difficulties. However, as many school systems have discovered, its benefits to the organization are worth the time and trouble.

The Forms of Cooperative Professional Development

Cooperative professional development is often confused with peer coaching, a system whereby teachers observe and confer with each other. However, as this author has pointed out (Glatthorn 1990), cooperative professional development is much more comprehensive than peer coaching. Its many forms are explained below as special components of cooperative development.

Peer Coaching

A review of the literature suggests that cooperative professional development most often takes the form of peer coaching or peer supervision. (The terms seem to be used interchangeably in the literature.) Goldsberry's (1986) "colleague consultation" model seems to be one of the most thorough and comprehensive. This author has simplified the Goldsberry model. First, the cooperative team sets up observational dyads, with both parties agreeing to observe each other twice during the school year. They hold an initial planning conference to share ideas about teaching and to decide on a tentative observational schedule. The teacher to be observed first identifies a focus for the observation. They select or develop a simple observational form to help the observer collect data on the observational focus. The observer makes the observation and records the data on the form. Then the observer becomes the observed; identifies the focus of the observation; and, with the help of the colleague, selects or develops an observational instrument.

After that first cycle of focused observations, they meet to exchange data. They examine the results of each focused observation, with the teacher observed determining the agenda and taking the lead in analyzing the data.

Observe several features about this approach. First, with the colleague acting as a facilitator and data source, the observed teacher controls the agenda: That person identifies the focus, determines the observational form, and takes charge of the debriefing. Because the one observed has all the power, the experience seems less threatening. Also note that the interactions have a clear focus. Rather than trying to replicate the entire supervisory cycle, the two colleagues focus on one aspect of their development where they want feedback. Finally, this approach, which emphasizes the analysis of focused data, reduces the likelihood that either member will slip into an evaluative mode.

Several sources present anecdotal evidence supporting the value of peer coaching. (See, for example, Dantonio 1995.) A few well-designed studies conclude that peer coaching had a positive effect on teachers' attitudes, encouraged them to experiment, improved communication, and helped them make specific changes in their teaching. (See Goldsberry 1986, Smyth 1983, Roper and Hoffman 1986, Sparks and Bruder 1987.) However, some evidence exists that peer coaching is beset with its own problems: Teachers who have not been trained to observe do not make reliable data sources, teachers in conference with each other tend to give excessive praise, and many teachers find the experience threatening. (See McFaul and Cooper's 1984 article and Goldsberry's [1984] response in the same issue.)

Professional Dialogues

Professional dialogues are structured discussions of professional issues designed to raise the level of teachers' cognition. As Clark and Peterson (1986) note, three aspects of a teacher's thinking play an important role in classroom performance: the teacher's theories and beliefs, the teacher's planning, and the teacher's interactive decision making while teaching. Professional dialogues are designed to influence all three.

Effective professional dialogues must be structured or they may degenerate into aimless talk. One model that this author has used successfully builds upon the work of Buchmann (1985).

The group meets initially to lay out a tentative schedule for the first three months, making preliminary decisions about the topics and assigning a leader for each discussion. The topics should meet three criteria: The topic is important to them professionally, the issues are ones about which informed professionals differ, and materials are available relating to the topic. Here is one list developed by a team of teachers:

- Learning styles
- Multicultural education
- Homework
- The hidden curriculum
- Inclusion of students with special needs

Each session follows a three-stage format. The first stage emphasizes external knowledge—information the experts have developed. The leader summarizes the research and the experts' recommendations, making sure the selected research is unbiased. For example, in a discussion of learning styles, the leader would include summaries of the research both supporting the accommodation of learning styles and questioning the usefulness of such accommodation. The members then analyze (not argue about) the external knowledge, asking such questions as these: To what extent do the experts agree? What are the specific issues that divide them? To what extent is the research reliable?

The second stage focuses on the personal knowledge of the members. They reflect on and share their experience about the topic. Because writing facilitates thinking, participants write about what they have learned from experience. The members then share their experiences and insights. Participants are encouraged to listen and not to dispute what has been said. They might ask the following questions of a teacher who reports great difficulty in accommodating learning styles:

• If you had homogeneous classes, would you have had those problems?

• Do you think you persisted long enough?

• Can you think of some simpler approach that would not involve developing special materials?

The intent of this stage is not to challenge the research but to draw upon the teachers' considerable experiential knowledge. At times, such knowledge will support the research, and at other times, it will question the research. In the latter case, teachers are encouraged to continue their inquiries and to persist in their reflections.

The third stage looks ahead and examines how knowledge from the discussion might affect planning and teaching. This stage enables each participant to arrive at a personal synthesis, linking the dialogues with future decision making. A teacher may continue studying the issue, continue with present practice that is now based upon a solid knowledge base, or change some aspect of teaching.

Although no empirical studies have concluded that teachers' behavior has changed because of such dialogues, some anecdotal evidence shows that participants have positive attitudes about the dialogues and report changes in their thinking as a consequence. (See Gibboney 1989, Welch 1994.)

Curriculum Development

Even in districts with developed curriculum guides that teachers are expected to use, much curriculum work still remains for the classroom teacher. As this author has noted (Glatthorn 1994), classroom teachers use the curriculum in several ways, and cooperative teams are probably the best structures for accomplishing this task:

• Develop yearly plans to implement the curriculum. Yearly plans show the units to be taught, the sequence in which they will be presented, and the amount of time they will require. Without a yearly plan, teachers can find the year has passed without major topics having been taught and time having been wasted. Although team members will make minor variations, team planning for the year builds a cohesive group of collaborators.

• Develop units of study based on the district curriculum guide. Unit planning is necessary because the unit best reflects a constructivist approach to learning. The unit also provides an excellent basis for lesson planning: Individual lessons should come from the unit instead of standing alone as isolated elements. A cooperative approach to unit planning results in quality units the team can share.

• Enrich the district curriculum. The district curriculum guide has probably been developed for all the students, perhaps making only general suggestions for individualizing content. Cooperative teams can pool special interests and knowledge to develop units that extend and deepen the required content for all learners.

• Provide for remediation. Some students cannot achieve mastery through the basic instruction. They need special materials that review key concepts, provide for alternative learning paths, and enable them to learn from tutors.

This use of the curriculum is a major contribution that cooperative teams can make to the overall success of the school.

Action Research

Action research (or teacher research) has gained increased attention in recent years, although Foshay (1994) traces its origins as far back as the 1940s, when Caswell founded the Horace Mann-Lincoln Institute of School Experimentation. Advocates have offered several definitions and typologies. The following definition is inclusive yet discriminating:

Systematic inquiry by practitioners (at times in collaboration with professors) into issues of educational practice, designed to deepen understanding and lead to interventions.

That systematic inquiry can use several research methods: documentation, document analysis, interviews, observations, and surveys. (Useful sources for explanations of specific methods are Sagor 1993, Hubbard and Power 1993.) The inquiry can examine several types of educational issues, including the following:

• The hidden curriculum or the culture of the school as it affects members.

• The written curriculum—the published curriculum materials.

• The supported curriculum—the texts, media, and software that support the curriculum.

• The tested curriculum—the means of assessing student learning.

• The taught curriculum—the curriculum as the teacher delivers it.

• The extra-curriculum—the activities programs and their effects.

• The professional behaviors of the researcher—how the principal administers, how the counselors confer with students, and how the teachers teach.

• The students—their special needs, talents, and behaviors.

• The parents and the community—their power, their attitudes about education, and their support of the schools.

Even though the processes will differ in relation to the issue and the method, this general problem-solving model has been found to be effective in this author's work with action research teams concerned with improving one aspect of schooling (see Glatthorn 1995):

1. Become aware of the mess, an ill-defined deficiency.
2. Study the mess to understand it better.
3. As a result of the study, define the problem.
4. Build the knowledge base with respect to the problem: Synthesize previous research and expert recommendations.
5. Generate creative solutions, drawing from both experiential and empirical knowledge.
6. Evaluate the solutions and design the intervention.
7. Implement the intervention and evaluate its effectiveness.

Several studies attest to the benefits of action research by practitioners. In their summary of the research, Cochran-Smith and Lytle (1990) note the following positive outcomes of teacher research: changes teacher-student relationships, develops the teacher's knowledge, improves teaching, fosters teacher reflection, facilitates collaboration, adds to the knowledge base, and provides an effective vehicle for teacher training. Teachers in the Tarboro (North Carolina) High School interviewed by this author reported that their action research deepened their understanding of school problems and enabled them to make major changes in the school's programs. Sagor (1991) concludes that schools with productive cultures will gain the most from action research; he adds that, even in schools where collaborative norms are weak, action research will do no harm.

However, Zeichner (1994) expresses several well-founded reservations about teacher research: It has not altered the balance of power between academics and practitioners; it has not always had a positive impact on teachers, but has in some cases provided support for undesirable practices; and it has not significantly changed institutions. This author would add this caveat based upon his experience: Much action research has too much action and too little research.

On balance, action research seems a useful way for teachers to collaborate, especially if they receive the necessary training and support.

Understanding the Operation of Cooperative Development

Each school will develop its own version of how this component operates. (See Chapter 8 for the steps to take in developing a home-grown model.) However, the following explanation describes how a typical model would operate:

1. The task force determines which components of the cooperative model will be available to teams. Flexibility is recommended here: Cooperative teams should be able to use any of the special components described above.

2. The task force orients teachers to the nature of the cooperative model, its benefits, its limitations, and its special components.

3. Each team meets with the principal to structure its cooperative work for the year ahead and to identify one major goal the team wishes to achieve. The goal should have professional significance and relate to the school improvement plan. The team also explains how it will achieve its goal and how it will demonstrate progress. A simple form like the one shown in Figure 5.1 (see p. 65) can be used to record these decisions.

4. The teams receive the staff development needed to acquire the special skills required by the components chosen.

5. Each team meets with the principal at the end of the year to review progress and to look ahead.

Ensuring the Success of Cooperative Development

Regardless of its form, cooperative professional development can effectively foster teacher growth only if certain steps are taken to ensure success:

1. Provide a supportive culture.
2. Ensure bottom-up involvement and top-down support.
3. Keep it simple.
4. Provide the needed training.
5. Arrange for the time needed.
6. Reward participants.

Figure 5.1: Sample Cooperative Development Form

Team: 7th grade math/science

Goal: Improve students' ability to solve math problems.

Steps to Achieve Goal

Our team will use our own combination of professional dialogues, peer coaching, and action research. We plan to proceed as follows:

1. Review research on mathematical problem solving.

2. Identify specific teaching methods that will foster math problem solving.

3. Write materials that other math teachers can use.

4. Use peer coaching to acquire and practice special teaching skills.

Methods for Demonstrating Progress

We hope we can show improved scores on the end-of-course math tests. However, we cannot guarantee that scores will show an increase this year. We will submit the following materials:

- A handbook for math teachers, including a review of the research on math problem solving and teaching techniques that increase problem-solving abilities.

- Teachers' reports on peer coaching experiences.

Provide a Supportive Culture.

Teacher growth should be anchored in a supportive culture based upon the values of collegiality, openness, and trust, as noted by Lieberman and Miller (1994). If the school values top-down decision making, isolation, and competition, the result will be what Hargreaves (1992) calls "contrived collegiality," which mandates that teachers cooperate to deal with administrative agendas. This author agrees with Hargreaves: Collegiality should develop naturally; however, certain structures and actions, as noted below, seem helpful.

Ensure Bottom-Up Involvement and Top-Down Support.

To avoid contrived collegiality, the cooperative program should be developed in a strategy that incorporates both "bottom-up" and "top-down" approaches. The substance and operational details of the program should be developed chiefly by the teachers so that they feel a sense of ownership. At the same time, both central office staff and school administrators must offer strong support. As Grimmett (1987) discovered, implementation of cooperative programs will probably be more effective with top-down encouragement and bottom-up involvement.

The principal must also play a key role as part of top-down support. The literature suggests that the principal should perform these functions in supporting the cooperative approach: Foster open communication among teachers, encourage teachers to share ideas, model and advocate learning as an ongoing process, provide needed resources, and publicly recognize and advocate for the program. (See Dantonio 1995, Ruck 1986.)

Keep It Simple.

The first responsibility of teachers is to teach effectively, and leaders must ensure that the cooperative program is not burdensome and unduly complicated. The program should be built upon existing team structures and not require the imposition of one more bureaucratic structure. Although enabling teachers from different grade levels and subject specializations to work together and exchange ideas has its virtue, such artificial teams do not seem to last very long. On the other hand, cooperative development activities that occur in an existing structure, such as a grade-level team or subject department, seem to last longer.

The need for simplicity also suggests that leaders should not complicate the program by requiring unnecessary paperwork. The principal can monitor the progress of the cooperative teams by holding brief conferences with the team during their planning period and by asking each team to present brief reports at faculty meetings.

Finally, cooperative programs will be more effective if they encourage teachers to focus on a small number of goals in their peer collaboration. For most cooperative teams, one or two major goals suffice. Teachers who must present several goals are tempted to identify trivial and easily accomplished outcomes.

Provide the Needed Training.

Cooperative teams must acquire the necessary special skills for the strategies they use. For example, teachers involved in peer observations must have the following skills:

- Setting the goals and clarifying the roles.
- Developing focused observation forms.
- Observing to collect focused observational data.
- Sharing focused observational data.

To achieve some economy of scale, such training programs can be planned and implemented at the district level. Or they can be presented at the school level, giving the teachers the resources necessary to conduct their own training.

Arrange for the Time Needed.

All models of supervision take time. However, the major limitation of cooperative professional development is that it takes more teacher time than any other approach. And, from the teachers' perspective, time is a priceless commodity. Schools that have made the cooperative approach effective have used several different strategies:

- Schedule common preparation periods for teachers.
- Change the daily schedule to accommodate peer collaboration: Start school late or dismiss early.
- Hire substitutes.
- Combine classes for large-group presentations.
- Arrange for special coverage of classes by supervisors and administrators.

Of all these options, the common preparation period causes the smallest incursion into instructional time, even though it may not give teachers the larger blocks of time needed for major projects.

Reward Participants.

The hope is that teachers will find that cooperative development results bring their own intrinsic rewards—satisfaction from professional growth, positive feelings of being part of a productive team, and knowledge that one's efforts bring about improvements in the organization. However, the extrinsic rewards of public recognition and praise also help.

References

Buchmann, M. (1985). "Improving Education by Talking: Argument or Conversation?" *Teachers College Record* 86, 3: 441–453.

Clark, C.M., and F.L. Peterson. (1986). "Teachers' Thought Processes." In *Handbook of Research on Teaching,* 3rd ed., edited by M.C. Wittrock. New York: Macmillan, pp. 255–296.

Cochran-Smith, M., and S.L. Lytle. (1990). "Research on Teaching and Teacher Research: The Issues That Divide." *Educational Researcher* 19, 2: 2–11.

Dantonio, M. (1995). *Collegial Coaching: Inquiry into the Teaching Self.* Bloomington, Ind.: Phi Delta Kappa.

Foshay, A.W. (1994). "Action Research: An Early History in the United States." *Journal of Curriculum and Supervision* 9, 4: 317–325.

Gibboney, R. (1989). "Just Words: Talking Your Way Past Reform to Educational Renewal." *Journal of Curriculum and Supervision* 4, 3: 230–245.

Glatthorn, A.A. (1990). *Supervisory Leadership.* New York: HarperCollins.

Glatthorn, A.A. (1994). *Developing the Quality Curriculum.* Alexandria, Va.: Association for Supervision and Curriculum Development.

Glatthorn, A.A. (1995). *Action Research: Scholarly Inquiry for School Improvement.* Greenville, N.C.: East Carolina University.

Goldsberry, L.F. (1984). "Reality—Really? A Response to McFaul and Cooper" *Educational Leadership* 41, 7: 10-11.

Goldsberry, L.F. (April 1986). "Colleague Consultation: Another Case of Fools Rush In." Paper presented at annual meeting of the American Educational Research Association, San Francisco, Calif.

Grimmett, P.P. (1987). "The Role of District Supervisors in the Implementation of Peer Coaching." *Journal of Curriculum and Supervision* 3, 1: 3-28.

Hargreaves, A. (1992). "Cultures of Teaching: A Focus for Change." In *Understanding Teacher Development,* edited by A. Hargreaves and M.G. Fullan. New York: Teachers College Press, pp. 216–240.

Hubbard, R.S., and B.M. Power. (1993). *The Art of Classroom Inquiry: A Handbook for Teacher-Researchers.* Portsmouth, N.H.: Heinemann.

Lieberman, A., and L. Miller. (1994). "Problems and Possibilities of Institutionalizing Teacher Research." In *Teacher Research and Educational Reform,* edited by S. Hollingsworth and H. Sockett. Chicago: University of Chicago Press, pp. 204–221.

McFaul, S.A., and J.M. Cooper. (1984). "Peer Clinical Supervision: Theory vs. Reality." *Educational Leadership* 41, 7: 4–9.

Roper, S.S., and D.E. Hoffman. (1986). *Collegial Support for Professional Improvement.* Eugene, Oreg.: Oregon School Study Council, University of Oregon.

Ruck, C.L. (1986). *Creating a School Context for Collegial Supervision: The Principal's Role as Contractor.* Eugene, Oreg.: Oregon School Study Council, University of Oregon.

Sagor, R. (1991). "What Project LEARN Reveals About Collaborative Action Research." *Educational Leadership* 48, 6: 6–10.

Sagor, R. (1993). *How to Conduct Collaborative Action Research.* Alexandria, Va.: Association for Supervision and Curriculum Development.

Smith, S.C., and J.J. Scott. (1990). *The Collaborative School: A Work Environment for Effective Instruction.* Eugene, Oreg.: ERIC Clearinghouse on Educational Management, University of Oregon.

Smyth, W. (April 1983). "Theory, Research, and Practice in Clinical Supervision." Paper presented at annual meeting of the American Educational Research Association, Houston.

Sparks, G.M., and S. Bruder. (April 1987). "How School-Based Peer Coaching Improves Collegiality and Experimentation." Paper presented at annual meeting of the American Educational Research Association, Washington, D.C.

Welch, O. (1994). "The Case for Inclusive Dialogue in Knowing, Teaching, and Learning About Multicultural Education." In *Teacher Research and Educational Reform,* edited by S. Hollingsworth and H. Sockett. Chicago: University of Chicago Press, pp. 52–66.

Zahorik, J.A. (1987). "Teachers' Collegial Interaction: An Exploratory Study." *Elementary School Journal* 87, 4: 385–396.

Zeichner, K.M. (1994). "Personal Renewal and Social Construction Through Teacher Research." In *Teacher Research and Educational Reform,* edited by S. Hollingsworth and H. Sockett. Chicago: University of Chicago Press, pp. 66–85.

6

Facilitating Self-Directed Development

Some experienced, competent teachers will prefer to work on their own to foster their professional development. For them, the self-directed development option should prove useful. This chapter presents a definition of and a rationale for self-directed development, reviews the models available, notes the conditions required for successful implementation of any self-directed model, and recommends a simplified model linked with school improvement.

Definition of and Rationale for Self-Directed Development

Self-directed development, as used in this book, is

A professional development process in which teachers work independently to foster their growth.

In contrast with intensive development, which requires the teacher to work with a supervisor, and different from cooperative development, which requires the teacher to work with a group of colleagues, self-directed development places teachers on their own. Although they will periodically interact professionally with administrators, supervisors, and other teachers, their professional development comes mainly through their individual initiatives.

The rationale for providing self-directed development rests on several bases. First, as Kilbourn (1991) notes, the argument can be made from a professional perspective. As he analyzes it, the concept of professionalism implies the responsibility of self-monitoring. Professionals, such as surgeons, attorneys, and architects, are expected to check closely on their own performance, making efforts to remain professionally current. Therefore, the current interest in professionalizing teaching, which emphasizes teacher autonomy, runs counter to the prevailing clinical model of supervision, which emphasizes reliance upon the supervisor.

Second, self-directed development reflects many of the principles of adult learning, as Loucks-Horsley and others (1987) point out. For adults, experience is the richest source of learning; self-directed development emphasizes analysis of and reflection on the teacher's experience. Also, adults desire increased autonomy with respect to their own learning; teachers in the self-directed mode are essentially autonomous, identifying their own growth goals, choosing the strategies to achieve those goals, and assessing their own progress.

Finally, self-directed development requires the least commitment of time, a scarce commodity for all teachers. Even though cooperative development probably has greater power to effect change through collaboration, many teachers are reluctant to work with colleagues because of the commitment of additional time.

Models of Self-Directed Development

All the specific models of self-directed development (many of which are identified by different names) involve several common elements. The teacher sets one or more growth goals for the year, develops a plan to achieve the goals, carries out the plan, and assesses and reports on progress. The supervisor plays a supportive role and does not take an active or controlling part.

One major way that self-directed models differ is in the source of the growth goals. Four sources for individual goals in the self-directed model are identified in the literature: professional roles, generic skills, subject-specific skills, and mixed sources.

Goals Based on Professional Roles

Several self-directed models take growth goals from an analysis of the professional role. For example, Redfern's (1980) "responsibility criteria" for teachers include 83 specific responsibilities for teachers, grouped into seven categories. The supervisor assists the teacher in identifying which of those responsibility areas needs development. Craft-Tripp (1993) analyzed the role of the special education supervisor and grouped activities into specific areas of responsibility. She then field-tested a self-directed, goal-based model in which these supervisors took their year's growth goal from one of the responsibility areas. Craft-Tripp's field test of the model concluded that the model was both feasible and effective. The supervisors preferred the self-directed model to their previous experiences with supervision.

Goals Based on the Generic Skills of Teaching

Several self-directed programs require teachers to derive the goal from a list of generic teaching skills seen as applicable to all subjects, all grades. Freiberg (1987) bases his "self-assessment" model on his Low Inference Self-Assessment Measure (LISAM), which includes six aspects of teaching: questioning skill, teacher talk–student talk, identification of set and closure, wait time, number of positive statements made by the teacher, and number of times the teacher uses student ideas.

The teacher makes an audiotape of a class and then does a self-assessment using the LISAM form. Then, the teacher can either collect additional data or work on one of the skills where development seems needed. Freiberg believes the following conditions are essential for success with this model: A climate to learn is present; teachers are interested in making changes; discussions about LISAM data are nonthreatening; staff development activities are provided; and the teacher sees a benefit to instructional development.

Goals Based on Subject-Specific Skills

Some experts in the field believe the goal should come from research on teaching a specific subject because most experienced teachers have mastered the generic skills and need challenge to develop subject-specific competencies. Hoover and Carroll (1987) based their program for reading teachers on a "Self-Assessment of Reading Group Instruction" form, which listed 10 research-based teacher behaviors in that area of instruction. Teachers made baseline tapes of two different reading groups within a two-week period. Then, they participated in a workshop on the targeted skills. Next, they analyzed their baseline tapes to identify the new skills they wished to acquire. After using the new approaches in their classrooms, they made two follow-up tapes, calling upon consultants when they needed help. The researchers' analysis of the teachers' pre- and post-test tapes indicated that the self-assessment procedure (followed by staff development) was an effective way to help teachers improve their skills.

Goals Based on Mixed Sources

Two models that use mixed sources seem worthy of note here. McGreal's (1983) "practical goal-setting approach" recommends four sources for identifying goals: organizational or administrative goals (e.g., "improve professional image"), program goals (e.g., "introduce new reading series"), learner goals (e.g., "students will demonstrate the ability to write a descriptive essay"), and teacher goals (e.g., "increase enthusiasm"). McGreal does not insist on measurable goals; he believes the judgments made by experienced supervisors and teachers are valid measures of improvement. Schools that have used this model report satisfaction; however, the burdens that it imposes on the principal have led McGreal to recommend that only one-third of the faculty be required to use the model each year.

Clark's (1992) model emphasizes the teachers as designers of their own professional development. He recommends that teachers design their own programs by using a seven-step process:

1. Write your own credo of teaching. Take your own beliefs seriously by making them explicit.
2. Start with your strengths; identify what you do well.
3. Make a five-year plan, which will give you a purpose and a sense of direction.
4. Focus on your own classroom as a place for your learning.
5. Ask for support.
6. Treat yourself, your colleagues, and your students with respect.
7. Let others know what you are doing.

Ensuring Successful Implementation of Self-Directed Models

Regardless of the model chosen, self-directed models seem to work effectively only with certain conditions and specific elements. The following recommendations are drawn from the literature on self-directed improvement:

1. Provide the necessary training for self-directed supervision. The following skills are essential:

• Set goals. Duke (1990) discovered that teachers experienced great difficulty in setting meaningful and challenging goals. He recommends that special attention be given to the framing of such goals.

• Develop professional development plans. Teachers will need help to develop realistic and effective plans to achieve the goals. Some teachers do not take the planning process seriously; others develop overly ambitious plans.

• Analyze tapes of one's own teaching. Teachers find that reviewing tapes of their teaching can be threatening and overwhelming. They will need help in knowing what to look for and how to record and use observations. The typical response to watching a tape of one's teaching is to focus on personal appearance or mannerisms, instead of noting significant teaching and learning behaviors. (See

Frager 1985 for an analysis of the difficulties of self-analyzing video-tapes.)

• Assess progress. Teachers also need help to make their own progress assessments and to secure feedback (see Item 4 below).

2. Keep the program simple. Many self-directed models have foundered because they were too complex: too many goals, too many conferences, and too much paperwork.

3. Provide the necessary resources. Provide funds for professional materials and conference attendance, and time for performing developmental activities.

4. Build in feedback processes. The major limitation of most self-directed models is the lack of feedback: The teachers work on their own, often in isolation, without using feedback from tape recordings, colleagues, students, or supervisors. The principal needs to stress the usefulness of feedback and insist the professional development plan include it in some form.

Student feedback is especially useful for teachers who work in the self-directed mode. However, certain cautions should be observed because such feedback is so controversial. First, student feedback should not be used in the formal teacher evaluation process without an explicit agreement to use it as one component of the evaluation process. Second, the teacher should not be required to discuss the results with a supervisor or administrator. Finally, the form used to solicit student feedback should be designed to minimize the evaluation of teaching and maximize the collection of useful feedback. One form many teachers have used successfully is shown in Figure 6.1 (see p. 76).

5. Encourage teachers to use processes that emphasize reflection. Developing the ability to reflect about one's teaching should be a primary goal of self-directed programs. Keeping a portfolio based upon reflective processes is one of the best ways of accomplishing that objective. This author's (Glatthorn 1996) work on teacher's portfolios explains in detail how the portfolio can play an instrumental role in fostering growth-oriented reflection.

Figure 6.1: Form for Student Feedback

Our Class: from the Students' Perspective

To the student:

Your teacher is interested in understanding how you see your class. You can help your teacher by completing this form. Consider each statement about your class. Decide to what extent you agree or disagree by circling one of the following at the end of the statement:

SA = strongly agree   **A** = agree   **D** = disagree   **SD** = strongly disagree

Remember, there are no right or wrong answers. And you are not being asked to evaluate your teacher. You are just telling your teacher how you see the class.

1.	We can understand the things we study in class.	SA	A	D	SD
2.	We seem to move at the right speed, not too fast or too slow.	SA	A	D	SD
3.	Our class has good discipline.	SA	A	D	SD
4.	Our teacher believes that we all can learn.	SA	A	D	SD
5.	The lessons seem well organized.	SA	A	D	SD
6.	We learn by doing interesting activities that keep us actively involved.	SA	A	D	SD
7.	We understand what the teacher explains.	SA	A	D	SD
8.	The teacher checks our learning and helps us correct mistakes.	SA	A	D	SD
9.	The teacher's questions help us think.	SA	A	D	SD
10.	I enjoy being in this class.	SA	A	D	SD

A Recommended Self-Directed Model

A review of the literature and analysis of experience working with several school systems have led this author to develop a simplified, self-directed model that includes the components noted above. The model operates as follows:

1. The principal and the faculty develop a school improvement plan. For example, a middle school faculty identified this as an improvement goal:

Students will demonstrate significant growth in reading ability.

2. Each teacher in the self-directed mode identifies one goal that derives from the school improvement plan. One science teacher identified this goal for the year:

Teach students the special reading skills they need in understanding science.

3. The teacher develops a tentative plan for achieving that goal and for demonstrating accomplishment. The plan should specify how feedback will be secured. The science teacher listed these activities:

• Review the research on reading in science to identify the skills needed.
• Confer with reading supervisor and science supervisor to secure their input.
• Develop five lessons focusing on the skills identified.
• Arrange for colleagues and supervisors to review and critique lesson plans; use their feedback to revise.
• Implement lesson plans.
• Get feedback from students on the lessons and use feedback to revise.
• Submit a final report documenting the steps taken and summarizing colleague and student feedback.

4. The teacher submits the plan to the principal for review. If the principal feels it necessary, the principal confers with the teacher.

5. The teacher implements the plan. If the teacher encounters problems, the teacher may request a conference with a supervisor or administrator.

6. The teacher submits a final report to the principal. If the teacher or the principal believes a conference is needed, they meet to review the report.

7. The teacher uses a portfolio to document the entire process, showing the results of reflection and self-analysis.

The model, although not yet rigorously tested, has several advantages that recommend it for serious consideration. First, it makes a direct connection between teacher development and school improvement. Second, it keeps the paperwork to a minimum and focuses teacher energy on one major development goal instead of on multiple goals. Finally, it simplifies the principal's role in the process: Conferences are held only when necessary.

References

Clark, C.M. (1992). "Teachers as Designers in Self-Directed Professional Development." In *Understanding Teacher Development*, edited by A. Hargreaves and M.G. Fullan. New York: Teachers College Press, pp. 75-84.

Craft-Tripp, M. (1993). "Self-Directed Development for Special Educators." Unpublished Ed.D. dissertation, North Carolina State University.

Duke, D. (1990). "Setting Goals for Professional Development." *Educational Leadership* 47, 8: 71-75.

Frager, A.M. (1985). "Video Technology and Teacher Training: A Research Perspective." *Educational Technology* 25, 7: 20-22.

Freiberg, H.J. (1987). "Teacher Self-Evaluation and Principal Supervision." *National Association of Secondary School Principals Bulletin* 71, 498: 85-92.

Glatthorn, A.A. (1996). *The Teacher's Portfolio*. Lancaster, Pa.: ProActive.

Hoover, N.L., and R.G. Carroll. (1987). "Self-Assessment of Classroom Instruction: An Effective Approach to Inservice Education." *Teaching and Teacher Education* 3, 3: 179-191.

Kilbourn, B. (1991). "Self-Monitoring in Teaching." *American Educational Research Journal* 28, 4: 721-736.

Loucks-Horsley, S., C.K. Harding, M.A. Arbuckle, L.B. Murray, C. Dubeq, and M.K. Williams. (1987). *Continuing to Learn*. Andover, Mass.: Regional Laboratory for Educational Improvement of the Northeast and the Islands.

McGreal, T.L. (1983). *Successful Teacher Evaluation*. Alexandria, Va.: Association for Supervision and Curriculum Development.

Redfern, G.B. (1980). *Evaluating Teachers and Administrators*. Boulder, Colo.: Westview.

The Evaluative Options in a Differentiated System

7

Providing Evaluative Options

Differentiated supervision works best when supported by a differentiated system for teacher evaluation. However, teacher evaluation provides only a supportive function and is not as important as teacher development. As Glickman (1991) notes in his review, teacher evaluation is not related to schoolwide instructional improvement. As Duke and Stiggins (1990) note, evaluation systems that mix accountability and professional growth may pose too much risk for the competent teacher, who decides to play it safe. However, the profession needs a fair and valid system for identifying incompetent teachers. The first section of this chapter presents an overview of evaluation models that promote growth; succeeding sections provide the details for this author's differentiated evaluation model.

Evaluation Systems That Promote Growth

Because of dissatisfaction with "score-card" systems of teacher evaluation, educators and scholars have recently turned their attention to developing and implementing evaluation systems that promote growth. Although the literature suggests widespread interest in such systems, Sando's (1995) survey of 200 midsize districts in California identified only nine districts that firmly believed their evaluation system promoted teachers' professional growth.

Despite the ambiguous data about the extent of interest, such systems seem to hold great promise when used with experienced, competent teachers. While varying in their particulars, most of these growth-oriented systems use a similar process:

1. The teacher identifies one or more growth goals; they may be multiyear goals. The principal reviews the goals in dialogue with the teacher.

2. The teacher uses several methods to make progress toward achieving the goals, such as reading, peer coaching, action research, graduate courses, and workshops.

3. The teacher solicits feedback about progress—from the principal, supervisor, colleagues, students, and parents.

4. The teacher prepares a portfolio that documents achievement.

5. The teacher does an annual self-assessment and confers with the principal for the formal evaluation.

Duke and Stiggins (1990) concluded from their study of effective systems that four elements seem essential: (1) mutual trust between teachers and administrators; (2) open channels of communication with a focus on improvement; (3) a strong commitment to the institution, to learning, and to improvement; and (4) clearly defined activities related to the evaluation process.

The Differentiated Evaluation Model

Evaluation systems that promote growth are similar to this author's "self-directed development"; the main difference is that the evaluation systems include a more rigorous evaluation process, perhaps minimizing their effectiveness as a development tool.

The differentiated evaluation system proposed here recognizes the limitations of and need for a professional evaluation system that emphasizes accountability; the differentiated supervision model emphasizes growth. The model proposed here makes a sharp distinction between two types of evaluation: intensive evaluation, designed to assist thc administrator in making personnel decisions (such as grant or deny tenure, renew or not renew contract, and promote or not promote); and standard evaluation, intended simply to comply with state or district requirements. For each of these options, this chapter provides an overview; readers interested in more detailed analyses of teacher evaluation should consult Millman and Darling-Hammond (1990).

Developing and Implementing Intensive Evaluation

As the term implies, intensive evaluation is a rigorous and intensive system of evaluating teachers according to districtwide criteria used with all teachers working in the intensive development mode: nontenured teachers and tenured teachers experiencing serious instructional problems. It emphasizes evaluation for purposes of accountability, not growth. A sequence of steps is recommended to conduct an intensive evaluation:

1. Ensure the presence of enabling conditions.
2. Develop legal and professional policies for teacher evaluation.
3. Analyze the teacher's role.
4. Identify criteria and processes for the essential skills of teaching.
5. Identify criteria and processes for the support skills.
6. Develop criteria for the administrative duties.
7. Provide the training needed for the evaluators.

Ensure the Presence of Enabling Conditions.

On the basis of their research, McLaughlin and Pfeifer (1988) identify four "enabling conditions" that should be present in the organization before a new system is introduced:

• **A Triggering Event That Calls Attention to the Need for a New System.** This event may take several forms: new leadership; a managerial crisis; or external pressures, such as a new state policy.

• **Strong Leadership at the District Level.** The superintendent plays a critical role in setting the process in motion, building board support, securing needed resources, providing substantive input, keeping the teachers' association informed, and monitoring the process.

• **Teacher Involvement.** Meaningful involvement of all teachers who wish to participate is essential; they need to feel a sense of ownership of the new system.

• **Environmental Stability.** The process of developing, testing, and implementing a new teacher evaluation system is a long-term set of operations, requiring several years. During that time, stability is important; radical changes in board membership, district leadership, and community relationships will cause too much turbulence.

Develop Legal and Professional Policies for Teacher Evaluation.

Because teacher evaluation can be troublesome when dismissal action is required, the district must have specific policies governing the evaluation process. The policies should be developed by a special task force composed of administrators, supervisors, and teachers and reviewed by the district's legal counsel to ensure compliance with the law.

Policies should deal with the following issues:

• The purposes of teacher evaluation.
• The evaluation options and how teachers are assigned to them.
• Those responsible for making evaluations. The individual responsible for evaluating teachers should not also provide developmental services; the two processes must be clearly separated.
• The processes, including the number of observations.
• The procedures to protect teachers' due process rights.
• The record-keeping and documentation system.

Analyze the Teacher's Role.

The intensive evaluation system begins with an analysis of the teacher's role. While minor variations occur periodically, the conceptualization shown in Figure 7.1 should cover most situations. As the figure indicates, the teacher is considered to have two primary roles: teaching, and performing administrative duties. The teaching role includes two sets of skills: the essential skills of teaching, observable in the classroom; and the support skills of teaching, not usually observable but crucial in supporting effective teaching.

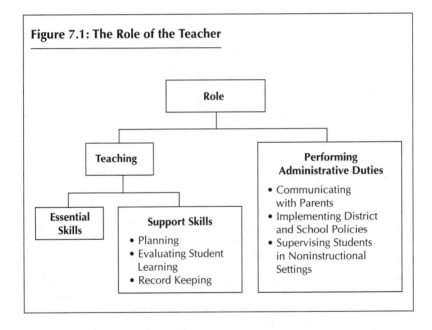

Figure 7.1: The Role of the Teacher

Identify Criteria and Processes for the Essential Skills of Teaching.

The criteria for intensive evaluation should be standardized for all subjects and grades across the district. The criteria should be drawn from the research on teacher effectiveness. Several formulations of such criteria are available. One set that has worked well for several districts is shown in Figure 7.2. In identifying criteria for intensive evaluation, developers should remember several cautions. First, avoid long lists of criteria; usually 8 to 12 are enough. Second, include only skills that make a difference. Avoid listing such criteria as "keeps attractive bulletin boards" or "dresses appropriately." Finally, be sure the list of essential skills includes only observable skills. "Develops effective plans," for example, should be included in the support skills. This distinction is important because different methods will be used for evaluating support skills (see the next section).

The teacher's effectiveness with the essential skills is best measured through a series of evaluative observations. District policies

---

Figure 7.2: Criteria for Essential Skills of Teaching

Lesson Content

1. Chooses lesson content that directly relates to curriculum goals, is appropriate in relation to student development, and is meaningful to students.

2. Presents content in a manner that demonstrates mastery of subject matter.

Classroom Climate

3. Creates a desirable learning environment that reflects appropriate discipline, supports instructional purposes, conveys high expectations, and keeps students on task.

4. Communicates realistically high expectations for all students.

5. Uses instructional time efficiently and effectively, allocating most of time available to curriculum-related activities and pacing instruction appropriately.

Instruction

6. Provides organizing structure for classroom work: reviews, provides overview, specifies objectives, gives clear directions, makes smooth transitions, summarizes, and achieves closure.

7. Uses appropriate learning activities for the objectives: demonstrates and explains clearly; provides for reinforcement through guided and independent practice.

8. Ensures active participation of all students in learning activities.

Assessment and Communication

9. Monitors student learning and uses evaluative data to adjust instruction.

10. Communicates effectively: explains clearly; questions effectively; and responds appropriately.

should specify the minimum number of evaluative observations. The research suggests that one or two observations do not provide sufficient representative data and 10 or more observations can become burdensome for both the teacher and the administrator. Also, Stodolsky (1990) concludes that the most valid evaluations will be based upon multiple observations of a representative sample of the teacher's teaching assignments. This finding is especially true for elementary teachers; in Stodolsky's study, elementary teachers seemed to vary in their effectiveness, depending upon the subject being taught.

Identify Criteria and Processes for the Support Skills.

Three separate criteria are needed for the support skills:

1. Makes effective plans for learning: develops yearly and unit plans.
2. Evaluates student learning: administers and uses the results of state and district tests; and develops and uses the results of valid teacher-made tests.
3. Maintains and uses accurate records of student attendance and achievement.

The teacher's performance of these support skills can best be measured through a special conference. The teacher is asked to bring the following documents: a yearly plan, a unit plan the teacher has developed, a test the teacher has given and graded, evidence that the teacher uses test results, and the teacher's class record book. The evaluator assesses the quality of these documents and discusses the teacher's performance of these support skills.

Develop Criteria for the Administrative Duties.

Three clear criteria are needed:

1. Communicates effectively with parents.
2. Implements district and school policies.
3. Supervises students effectively in noninstructional settings.

The assessment of the teacher's performance of these administrative duties is best made by compiling and analyzing anecdotal reports collected over the year. Any time the administer has direct evidence of excellent or unsatisfactory performance of these duties, an anecdotal report should be written, shared with the teacher, and maintained in the teacher's personnel file.

Provide the Training Needed for the Evaluators.

Intensive training should be provided for those who evaluate teachers. The training sessions should deal with the following issues:

1. Implementing district policies.
2. Conducting and documenting evaluation observations.
3. Holding conferences based upon evaluation observations.
4. Evaluating the support skills.
5. Keeping and using anecdotal records.
6. Providing remediation to teachers who are marginal performers.
7. Making summative evaluations.
8. Following due process dismissal procedures.

Four of these issues perhaps need special attention:

• *Evaluation observations* have a special purpose and structure. First, most of the evaluation observations should be unannounced to ensure that the observer is not seeing a rehearsed performance. The observer should remain for a full instructional period, making a complete and time-based record of all significant teaching-learning transactions. At the end of the observation, the observer should make a holistic assessment of the teacher's performance: Was the lesson satisfactory or unsatisfactory? Then, as soon as possible after the observation, the observer should review the detailed notes and then record an analytic rating for each skill. The observer should use a standard form that lists the essential skills, provides space for a rating for each skill, and has space for noting the evidence that supports the rating.

In scheduling formal evaluation observations for novice teachers, administrators should keep in mind Reynold's (1992) recommendation that formal evaluations for such teachers should not begin until after the middle of the first year. Her review of the literature leads her to conclude that novices will need the first term to learn about the school and its culture. At the same time, administrators face the pressures of making contract decisions by early April.

• *Conferences based on evaluation observations* should be characterized by directness and specificity. The teacher knows that the purpose of the observation was to evaluate, not develop. The teacher has been oriented to the criteria and the use of the evaluation form. Thus, the teacher's burning question is, "How did I do?" Therefore, the recommendation is that the observer should begin with a direct statement of the holistic rating; for example, "I judged your performance as unsatisfactory." Then the evaluator should review the analytic ratings, providing specific evidence for each assessment. The conference should conclude with the evaluator explaining what remediation will be offered and involve the teacher in the completion of a professional development plan. Throughout this conference, the teacher should review both the evaluation form and the observer's notes.

Those who question the wisdom of such a direct conference should consider the analogy of the gymnast at a gym meet. The gymnast performs the routine and turns to the judges. The judges hold up a score card. They do not ask, "How did you feel about that routine?"

• *The remediation* should be carefully planned and implemented. The professional development plan should specify the following: the skills to be remediated, the processes to be used, the professional who will provide the remediation, and the date a progress report is required. The recommendation is for the principal or assistant principal to conduct the evaluation process; a mentor should provide the remediation. In implementing the professional development plan for remediation, the mentor should use the processes identified for intensive development, giving special emphasis to coaching. Careful documentation of how the plan was implemented is essential, especially if dismissal seems probable.

• *The summative evaluation* should be a holistic assessment of the teacher's ability at the time the final evaluation is made and not an averaging of all the observation assessments. The summative evaluation should answer this question: "At the time this summative evaluation was made, was the teacher's overall performance satisfactory or unsatisfactory?" Obviously, the teacher's mastery of the essential skills should be the primary consideration, although the evaluations of the support skills and the administrative duties should also be factored in.

Those interested in more information about working with the incompetent teacher should consult Bridges (1992) and Glatthorn (1996a).

Developing and Implementing Standard Evaluations

Standard evaluations comply with state or district requirements that all teachers be evaluated and are provided only to those teachers whose performance is known to be fully satisfactory. Standard evaluations are not intended to provide data for administrative decisions.

In the process recommended here, the teacher completes a self-assessment report, summarizing accomplishments through the cooperative or the self-directed mode. In some districts, the self-assessment is recorded in a comprehensive portfolio. (See Glatthorn 1996b for further details about the use of the portfolio in teacher evaluation.) The principal reviews the self-assessment and, if a conference seems necessary, confers with the teacher to discuss progress achieved that year and goals proposed for the next year. They both sign the official form.

Obviously, standard evaluation as recommended here is a formality without impact on professional development, which will come about through the developmental options.

References

Bridges, E.M. (1992). *The Incompetent Teacher: Managerial Responses.* Washington, D.C.: Falmer.

Duke, D.L., and R.J. Stiggins. (1990). "Beyond Minimum Competence: Evaluation for Professional Development." In *The New Handbook of Teacher Evaluation,* edited by J. Millman and L. Darling-Hammond. Newbury Park, Calif.: Sage, pp. 116–132.

Glatthorn, A.A. (1996a). *Quality Teaching Through Professional Development.* Thousand Oaks, Calif.: Corwin.

Glatthorn, A.A. (1996b). *The Teacher's Portfolio.* Lancaster, Pa.: ProActive.

Glickman, C. (1991). "Pretending Not to Know What We Know." *Educational Leadership* 48, 8: 4–10.

McLaughlin, M.W., and R.S. Pfeifer. (1988). *Teacher Evaluation.* New York: Teachers College Press.

Millman, J., and L. Darling-Hammond, eds. (1990). *The New Handbook of Teacher Evaluation.* Newbury Park, Calif.: Sage.

Reynolds, A. (1992). "What Is Competent Beginning Teaching? A Review of the Literature." *Review of Educational Research* 62, 1: 1–35.

Sando, J.P. (1995). "Implementation of Teacher Evaluation Systems That Promote Professional Growth." Unpublished doctoral dissertation, University of Southern California, Los Angeles.

Stodolsky, S.S. (1990). "Classroom Observation." In *The New Handbook of Teacher Evaluation,* edited by J. Millman and L. Darling-Hammond. Newbury Park, Calif.: Sage, pp. 175–190.

Building Homegrown
Differentiated Models

8

Developing the Local Model

Rather than prescribing a single model of differentiated supervision, this author recommends a process approach in which each school or district develops its own model responsive to its own needs and resources. The process explained below has been successful with several school districts:

1. Appoint a task force for teacher development. The task force should be a representative group of 10 to 15 members—small enough to be efficient and large enough to be representative. The following constituencies should be represented: district administrators, district supervisors, school administrators, department chairs or team leaders, and classroom teachers. Lay representation may be included if desirable. The task force should have a budget to secure necessary resources, such as professional books, videotapes, conferences, and consultant advice. A reasonable deadline for the task force's recommendations should be set.

Also, the scope of the task force's responsibility should be clearly delineated. Is it developing guidelines for a total system of professional development (including staff development, teacher evaluation, and informal observations), or is its work limited to individual development? The steps given here focus on the individual development option, although those other components could also be included.

2. Inform the teachers. To allay anxiety and reduce rumor-mongering, the superintendent should inform all teachers about the goals and scope of the project, assuring them they will have an opportunity to provide input and that their contract will be honored. The superintendent's message should be followed by faculty meetings at the school level in which the principal can give the same assurances.

3. Develop the knowledge base. The task force should develop its own knowledge base by reading the relevant literature, attending related conferences and workshops, visiting nearby schools with similar systems, and getting input from consultants. As the members acquire knowledge, they should summarize it in reports for their own use and possible subsequent use by administrators and teachers.

4. Determine the balance between district control and school autonomy. In consultation with the superintendent, the task force should next determine this key issue. Three choices are available: (1) the district will implement one uniform system for all schools; (2) the district will establish uniform guidelines about essential policies but give schools considerable autonomy; and (3) each school may develop its own system. Although district size will affect the choice, providing some school autonomy within district guidelines seems most effective because it respects the need for district control and standardization while giving schools some latitude in developing their own programs.

5. Develop the basic policies that will govern the operation of the differentiated system. The task force should begin the process of policy development by framing an initial version that deals with key issues. One set of policy statements is presented in Figure 8.1 (see p. 97) to illustrate the kinds of issues that should be addressed. Observe that it reflects the position recommended above: Individual schools have some autonomy within general district guidelines.

6. Determine how tenured teachers will receive options. One policy matter that needs special consideration involves the tenured teachers—those new to the district and those with previous experience in

the district. Tenured teachers new to the district can be dealt with in two ways. Some districts prefer to assign them to the intensive mode until they have demonstrated their competence. Other districts prefer to give them a choice of cooperative or self-directed development, until evidence shows that the intensive mode is needed. Remember, a

Figure 8.1: Policies Recommended for the Differentiated System

The Central School District has adopted a differentiated system to improve its schools by professionalizing the supervision of its teachers. The following policies govern its operation:

1. All provisions of the differentiated system will be in accordance with the state school code, be consonant with other school district policies, will honor the bargaining agreement between the school board and the teachers' association, and will respect the teachers' rights for due process.

2. All teachers must participate in staff development; all teachers will be evaluated; all teachers will experience informal observations by administrators or supervisors.

3. All probationary teachers must participate in the intensive development (or clinical supervision) program until they have gained tenure. If they wish, they may supplement the intensive approach with another component.

4. Teachers who believe they have been inappropriately assigned to any of the developmental programs should first request review by the principal and then, if not satisfied, request a similar review by the director of personnel. Teachers still dissatisfied with the decision may use the established grievance procedures for further appeal.

5. Each school faculty, in cooperation with its principal, will develop its specific differentiated program. All such programs will comply with these policy provisions. All schools will receive the same proportional share of the professional development budget to implement the program.

6. School board policies will govern any differentiated program that requires release time for teachers or coverage of classes by substitutes or nonprofessional staff.

7. The assistant superintendent for instruction will coordinate, direct, and monitor the entire program, and submit reports to the superintendent of schools.

8. District supervisors are expected to play an important role in each school's intensive development program, subject to their availability and the principal's determination of need. District supervisors may also assist in the implementation and facilitation of the other developmental modes.

teacher can work in two modes; for example, a tenured teacher needing major assistance could be assigned to work in the intensive mode but could choose to use the cooperative model as well.

In deciding on options for experienced teachers who have been with the school district, two choices again are available. Some districts have decided that all teachers, regardless of tenure or competence, should experience some intensive development. They divide these teachers into three or four cohorts, usually by asking teachers to express a preference, and then cycle the cohorts through the intensive mode. Cohort 1 experiences the intensive mode during the first year of operation; Cohort 2, the second year; and so on. During the off years, tenured, competent teachers have a choice of cooperative or self-directed development. Tenured teachers who are perceived as marginal performers would be required to join Cohort 1 and would then remain in the intensive mode until the principal or supervisor no longer determined any need for it.

The other option is to let all tenured teachers express a preference for the development mode, with the principal retaining a veto right. Here, the principal can require a marginal tenured teacher to participate in the intensive mode even if that teacher prefers another. These decisions about tenured teachers should also be translated into proposed policies that would be added to an existing set of policies (such as those in Figure 8.1).

7. Clarify roles. With general policy guidelines set, the task force should then make a tentative decision about the roles of district and school personnel in implementing the program. One system for making such a determination is to use the role/function matrix shown in Figure 8.2 (see p. 99). On the left are the important functions in implementing the program, and across the top are roles that could be involved. After in-depth discussion, the task force would complete the form, indicating who would be primarily responsible for each function and who would contribute.

8. Present proposed policies for review and discussion. A tentative version of the policies should be presented to and reviewed by all administrators, supervisors, and teachers. Build strong support for the

Figure 8.2: Form for Function/Role Analysis in Differentiated Supervision

Differentiated Program Function	ROLE				
	Asst. Super-intendent	District Supervisor	Principal or Asst. Principal	School Supervisor	Expert Teacher
Administer district program.					
Evaluate district program.					
Administer school program.					
Evaluate school program.					
Provide clinical supervision.					
Facilitate cooperative model.					
Facilitate self-directed node.					

Directions: Insert the letter **R** in the appropriate cell to indicate who will be primarily responsible for a particular function; insert the letter **C** to indicate who will contribute to that function.

program at the start by ensuring that all constituencies have an opportunity to ask questions, discuss issues, and make recommendations.

9. Provide staff development to help schools develop their own programs. With those policies clearly established, school administrators and teachers will need staff development and technical assistance as

they formulate their own programs. Staff development should deal with the following professional issues:

- Advantages and limitations of self-directed and cooperative programs.
- Varieties and benefits of each self-directed approach.
- Varieties and benefits of each cooperative approach.
- Skills required to implement self-directed and cooperative approaches.
- Development of a school-based differentiated program.

Each faculty, under the leadership of its principal, would develop its own differentiated program, describing its operation in a proposal to the task force. In addition to describing the specific options for teachers, the proposal also indicates specific roles that school leaders would have in implementing the program at the school level.

10. Provide for formative and summative evaluation of the program. The task force should also develop explicit guidelines for formative and summative evaluation at both the district and school levels. Two kinds of formative assessments are useful. First, those involved in the self-directed and cooperative modes should submit progress reports to the principal, noting accomplishments and identifying problems. Second, the principal should monitor overall progress by meeting periodically with teams or individuals to assess their responses to the program and to do any needed troubleshooting. The principal should submit a written progress report to the task force, summarizing personal assessments and those of the teachers.

Summative evaluation is needed to make general assessments of the program's effectiveness and to determine the need for any major changes. Note, however, that researchers who have studied the change process warn against premature summative evaluation. (See Seidman 1983.) This caution suggests that the task force may wish to rely upon formative evaluation alone during the first year, deferring summative evaluation until the second year. The summative evaluation can be based on several methods and sources of data: surveys of perceptions of administrators, supervisors, and teachers; interviews with principals, supervisors, and a sampling of teachers; and compilation and analysis of progress reports.

11. Develop a budget proposal for implementing the program. Funds will be required for staff development, professional materials, and conference attendance. In addition, some districts have found it useful to provide for substitutes to support the cooperative mode.

12. Initiate the program, following the guidelines for effective program implementation. With these planning processes completed, the program is ready for initiation and implementation. Leaders should remember the research-based recommendations on effective implementation: Be sensitive to the changing concerns of teachers; provide needed resources; provide on-going staff development; secure active support of school principals; maintain pressure on teachers to carry out the new program effectively; and monitor the program and solve emerging problems. (See Fullan's 1991 review.)

Through this process, school districts can develop their own differentiated model that responds to their needs and makes the most effective use of their resources.

If evaluative options are offered, then similar issues need to be addressed. The following issues involving intensive evaluation need special attention:

- Who will be assigned to intensive evaluation? The recommendation is that all nontenured teachers and all tenured teachers experiencing serious problems be assigned to this track, unless the district decides to cycle cohorts through the intensive evaluation program.

- Who will be responsible for intensive evaluation? The school administrator should be responsible.

- What criteria will be used? The district should develop its own criteria unless state criteria are required.

- What evidence is required? The policies should specify the minimum number of observations and conferences, and other data to be gathered and used.

- Who will carry out the remediation plan? A mentor or supervisor is the most effective.

• By what process will teachers move from the intensive to the standard track? The principal can determine this and report the decision to the personnel office.

Standard evaluation poses less of a problem. The program should specify the following: who is eligible for this track; who carries out the responsibility; how many observations are required; and how reassignment takes place.

Concluding Note

Homegrown models responsive to district strengths and needs seem to work best. The schools listed in the Appendix are a useful resource, however, for districts that want to learn from those with experience in developing their own model.

References

Fullan, M.G. (1991). *The New Meaning of Educational Change*. New York: Teachers College Press.

Seidman, W.H. (1983). "Goal Ambiguity and Organizational Decoupling: The Failure of 'Rational Systems' Program Implementation." *Educational Evaluation and Policy Analysis* 5, 4: 399–413.

Appendix: Schools Using the Differentiated Model

In response to a published query, the following schools report that they are using their own form of differentiated supervision and that they are willing to share their experiences with the model. Other schools that have developed their own version of differentiated supervision are asked to contact the author at Speight Building, East Carolina University, Greenville NC 27858. In each case, the school or school system using some form of differentiated supervision is noted below, along with the name of the primary contact person. In some instances, there may be a small charge for materials.

Connecticut
Branford Public Schools
1111 Main Street,
Branford, CT 06405
Bruce E. Storm, Superintendent

Illinois
Sycamore Community Schools
245 West Exchange Street
Sycamore, IL 60178
Robert L. Hammon, Superintendent

Township High School District 113
1040 Park Avenue West
Highland Park, IL 60035
Arnold Barbknecht, Executive Director for Instruction

Iowa
Lewis Central Community School District
1600 East South Omaha
Bridge Road
Council Bluffs, IA 51503
James Veriengia, Superintendent

Maine
Wells High School
Box 579, Sanford Road
Wells, ME 04090
Valjeane M. Olenn, Principal

Massachusetts
Gill Montague Regional School District
Crocker Avenue
Turners Falls, MA 01376
Anthony Serio, Superintendent

Minnesota
School District 112
1700 Chestnut Street
Chaska, MN 55318
David St. Germain, Superintendent

New York
Baldwin Union Free School District
960 Hastings Street
Baldwin, NY 11510
Kathy Weiss, Superintendent

Levittown Public Schools
Abbey Lane
Levittown, NY 11756
Roberta A. Gerold, Assistant Superintendent for Instruction

Onteora Junior Senior High School
Boiceville NY 12412
Francis J. Gorleski, Jr., Principal

North Carolina
Tarboro High School
1400 Howard Avenue
Tarboro, NC 27886
Lana J. VanderLinden, Principal

Pennsylvania
Central Dauphin School District
600 Rutherford Road
Harrisburg, PA 17109
John S. Herigan, Administrative Assistant, Elementary Education

Dauphin County Technical School
6001 Locust Lane
Harrisburg, PA 17109
Robert W. Clark, Assistant Director

Vermont
Brattleboro Union High School
50 Fairground Road
Brattleboro, VT 05301
Daniel A. Heller, Director of Professional Development

Wisconsin
Sheboygan Area School District
830 Virginia Avenue
Sheboygan, WI 53081
Marlin L. Tanck, Director of Instructional Services

Orange Windsor Supervisory Union
Box 240
South Royalton, VT 05068
Robert M. Carchman, Superintendent

Canada, British Columbia
School District 14
Bag 5000
Oliver, BC, Canada V0H 1TO
Brian Fox, Assistant Superintendent of Schools

Canada, Manitoba
Brandon School Division
Brandon, MB, Canada R7B 2N8
V. Lois Ross, King George School